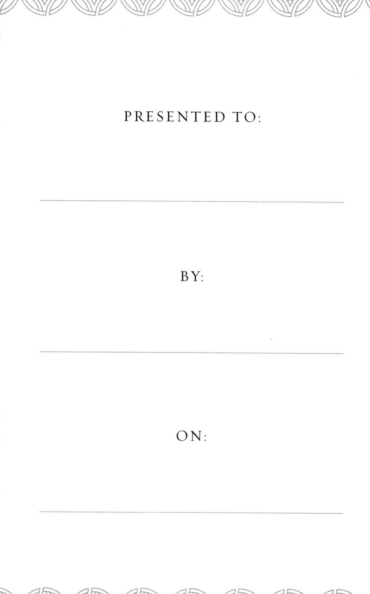

PRESENTED TO:

....

BY:

....

ON:

....

God's Book of Proverbs
of Proverbs
for Graduates

Biblical Wisdom Arranged *by* Topic

PUBLISHING GROUP

NASHVILLE, TENNESSEE

ISBN: 978-1-4627-7823-2

Editorial & Interior Design and Typesetting: Hudson
Bible (HudsonBible.com)

Printed in China
RRD
18 19 20 21 22 · 8 7 6 5 4 3 2

Table of Contents

God's Book of Proverbs

Connecting Wisdom to Jesus

The book you hold is filled with wisdom from God.
It contains every proverb in the Bible—a collection of
divinely inspired words that have informed and guided
people for thousands of years.

Our world could certainly use a dose of biblical wisdom. We live in an information age where technology
keeps us connected to others and up to speed on current
events during every waking moment. In this flood of
information, however, wisdom gets lost. Wisdom is the
type of knowledge you can't look up on Wikipedia; it
only comes from following God's guidance as we navi-
gate the world he has made.

We don't need more information; we need more
wisdom.

This book of Proverbs, topically arranged, is designed
to give you God's guidance in matters related to every-
day life. Covering finances, speech, friends, and more,
the Proverbs urge us to stop and listen, considering our
father's instruction and not rejecting the teaching of our
mother (Pr 1:8-9). The Proverbs challenge us to learn
from those who have gone before us.

You will find ancient guidance in this little book of
biblical wisdom. Do not think, however, that in learning
to be wise you can find happiness and salvation.

King Solomon, the man responsible for most of the

sayings in this book, was considered the wisest man in history. He asked God not for wealth or power, but for wisdom so he could judge fairly as king (1Kg 3:1-15). God honored his request and made Solomon wise.

Even so, Solomon disregarded some of the wisdom God gave him. Toward the end of his life, he allowed his heart to be led astray. He acquired many wives. He followed their gods and worshipped their idols. Even with all his wisdom, he still fell short.

The same is true for us. While we can receive the wisdom of this book, wisdom in itself will not save us. It will not keep us from doing wrong, hurting others, or hurting ourselves.

Thus we need wisdom with a capital W—we need Wisdom as a Person to save us. The New Testament, picking up where the Old Testament leaves off, emphasizes "something greater than Solomon is here" (Lk 11:31).

In his teaching and preaching, Jesus of Nazareth displayed the wisdom of God. From the way he responded when confronted with difficult questions to the way he discerned what was in the hearts of those around him, Jesus showed himself to be the ultimate example of wisdom.

The Bible reveals Jesus as more than just an example, however. He is also the Savior. He was greater than Solomon not only because he exceeded the ancient king in wisdom, but also because he gave us the ultimate gift of love: his life.

The Apostle Paul, writing just a few decades after the death and resurrection of Jesus, proclaimed that "Christ Jesus . . . became wisdom from God for us" (1Co 1:30). Jesus is our wisdom. Salvation comes not from acquiring knowledge about the world but from knowing the God who made the world. Jesus made this possible for everyone.

The entire message of the Bible, including this book of Proverbs, is summarized like this: God made a good world. People made choices that tainted the world with human sin and evil. But "God loved the world in this way: He gave his one and only son, so that everyone who believes in him will not perish but have eternal life" (Jn 3:16). By turning from our sin and trusting in Jesus, the one who became wisdom from God for us, we can know true wisdom now and be assured of living in God's presence forever.

This little book of Proverbs offers you wisdom and points to the only one who can satisfy and save you.

Trevin Wax

Bible and Reference Publisher
at LifeWay Christian Resources
and general editor of The Gospel Project

How to Read
God's Book of Proverbs

This book is a browser's delight. More than a book to read, it's an index to search. You have two ways to search:

1. Check the alphabetical sections.
2. Investigate the index.

Want to know about money? Refer to the money section. Eager to see what Proverbs says about relationships? Use the index to guide you to the right pages. Then you might wonder about the source of true happiness, so go on a new search. Consequently you might ponder what kinds of relationships lead to happiness, so the happiness entry sends you to friendships, to marriage, and to how to resolve conflict within each.

As you read, you might mark your book by circling favorites in each section, by marking your own cross-references, and by noting in the margin a way you have applied each proverb.

Understanding parallelism will enhance your comprehension of the proverbs. Parallelism is the idea of repeated or expanded thoughts from one line to the next, a common feature of ancient poetry. Proverbs, along with Psalms and other wisdom books such as Ecclesiastes and the Song of Solomon, are examples of poetic literature.

Antithetical parallelism makes its point by pairing two opposing ideas. We see this in Proverbs 12:16: "A fool's displeasure is known at once, but whoever ignores an insult is sensible."

Synonymous parallelism restates an idea to emphasize a point. Proverbs 19:5 is an example: "A false witness will not go unpunished, and one who utters lies will not escape."

Finally, synthetic parallelism builds upon a thought, with a second line that adds to the idea. This is presented in Proverbs 14:7: "Stay away from a foolish person; you will gain no knowledge from his speech." As you travel through Proverbs, keep an eye out for the parallelism used and for what this literary technique does to enhance the meaning of the text.

In his article "Introduction to Proverbs," Bible teacher Bob Deffinbaugh says the proverbs will challenge us as readers: "We are not given all the data, but what is given heightens our interest and our imagination. . . . That is a part of the genius of the proverb."

Anger

"A wise person is cautious and turns from evil,
but a fool is easily angered and is careless."

Proverbs 14:16

A gentle answer turns away anger,
but a harsh word stirs up wrath.

Proverbs 15:1

A hot-tempered person stirs up conflict,
but one slow to anger calms strife.

Proverbs 15:18

A king's fury is a messenger of death,
but a wise person appeases it.

Proverbs 16:14

A person's own foolishness leads him astray,
yet his heart rages against the LORD.

Proverbs 19:3

A king's rage is like the roaring of a lion,
but his favor is like dew on the grass.

Proverbs 19:12

A person with intense anger bears the penalty;
if you rescue him, you'll have to do it again.

Proverbs 19:19

A king's terrible wrath is like the roaring of a lion;
anyone who provokes him endangers himself.

Proverbs 20:2

A secret gift soothes anger,
and a covert bribe, fierce rage.

Proverbs 21:14

The one who sows injustice will reap disaster,
and the rod of his fury will be destroyed.

Proverbs 22:8

Don't make friends with an angry person,
and don't be a companion of a hot-tempered one,
or you will learn his ways
and entangle yourself in a snare.

Proverbs 22:24-25

A person who does not control his temper
is like a city whose wall is broken down.

Proverbs 25:28

Fury is cruel, and anger a flood,
but who can withstand jealousy?

Proverbs 27:4

Mockers inflame a city,
but the wise turn away anger.

Proverbs 29:8

A fool gives full vent to his anger,
but a wise person holds it in check.

Proverbs 29:11

An angry person stirs up conflict,
and a hot-tempered one increases rebellion.

Proverbs 29:22

If you have been foolish by exalting yourself
or if you've been scheming,
put your hand over your mouth.

For the churning of milk produces butter,
and twisting a nose draws blood,
and stirring up anger produces strife.

Proverbs 30:32-33

Beauty

She [Understanding] will place a garland of favor on
your head; she will give you a crown of beauty.

Proverbs 4:9

Don't lust in your heart for her beauty
or let her captivate you with her eyelashes.
For a prostitute's fee is only a loaf of bread,
but the wife of another man goes after a precious life.

Proverbs 6:25-26

A beautiful woman who rejects good sense
is like a gold ring in a pig's snout.

Proverbs 11:22

A house is built by wisdom,
and it is established by understanding;
by knowledge the rooms are filled
with every precious and beautiful treasure.

Proverbs 24:3-4

A word spoken at the right time
is like gold apples in silver settings.
A wise correction to a receptive ear
is like a gold ring or an ornament of gold.

Proverbs 25:11-12

Charm is deceptive and beauty is fleeting,
but a woman who fears the LORD will be praised.

Proverbs 31:30

Calamity

Since I [Wisdom] called out and you refused,
extended my hand and no one paid attention,
since you neglected all my counsel
and did not accept my correction,
I, in turn, will laugh at your calamity.
I will mock when terror strikes you,
when terror strikes you like a storm
and your calamity comes like a whirlwind,
when trouble and stress overcome you.

Proverbs 1:24-27

At the end of your life, you will lament
when your physical body has been consumed,

and you will say, "How I hated discipline,
and how my heart despised correction.
I didn't obey my teachers
or listen closely to my instructors.
I am on the verge of complete ruin
before the entire community."

Proverbs 5:11-14

He always plots evil with perversity in his heart;
he stirs up trouble.
Therefore calamity will strike him suddenly;
he will be shattered instantly, beyond recovery.

Proverbs 6:14-15

The wise store up knowledge,
but the mouth of the fool hastens destruction.

Proverbs 10:14

When the whirlwind passes,
the wicked are no more,
but the righteous are secure forever.

Proverbs 10:25

The way of the LORD is a stronghold for the honorable,
but destruction awaits the malicious.

Proverbs 10:29

The one who searches for what is good seeks favor,
but if someone looks for trouble, it will come to him.

Proverbs 11:27

By rebellious speech an evil person is trapped,
but a righteous person escapes from trouble.

Proverbs 12:13

No disaster overcomes the righteous,
but the wicked are full of misery.

Proverbs 12:21

The one who guards his mouth protects his life;
the one who opens his lips invites his own ruin.

Proverbs 13:3

A wicked envoy falls into trouble,
but a trustworthy courier brings healing.

Proverbs 13:17

Disaster pursues sinners,
but good rewards the righteous.

Proverbs 13:21

The house of the righteous has great wealth,
but trouble accompanies the income of the wicked.

Proverbs 15:6

The one who mocks the poor insults his Maker,
and one who rejoices over calamity
will not go unpunished.

Proverbs 17:5

The one who sows injustice will reap disaster,
and the rod of his fury will be destroyed.

Proverbs 22:8

My son, fear the LORD, as well as the king,
and don't associate with rebels,
for destruction will come suddenly from them;
who knows what distress these two can bring?

Proverbs 24:21-22

Don't abandon your friend or your father's friend,
and don't go to your brother's house
in your time of calamity;
better a neighbor nearby than a brother far away.

Proverbs 27:10

Happy is the one who is always reverent,
but one who hardens his heart falls into trouble.

Proverbs 28:14

One who becomes stiff-necked,
after many reprimands
will be shattered instantly—
beyond recovery.

Proverbs 29:1

Conflict

The LORD hates six things;
in fact, seven are detestable to him:
arrogant eyes, a lying tongue,
hands that shed innocent blood,
a heart that plots wicked schemes,
feet eager to run to evil,
a lying witness who gives false testimony,
and one who stirs up trouble among brothers.

Proverbs 6:16-19

Hatred stirs up conflicts,
but love covers all offenses.

Proverbs 10:12

The one who conceals hatred has lying lips,
and whoever spreads slander is a fool.

Proverbs 10:18

Arrogance leads to nothing but strife,
but wisdom is gained by those who take advice.

Proverbs 13:10

Fools mock at making reparation,
but there is goodwill among the upright.

Proverbs 14:9

A gentle answer turns away anger,
but a harsh word stirs up wrath.

Proverbs 15:1

Better a meal of vegetables where there is love
than a fattened ox with hatred.

Proverbs 15:17

A hot-tempered person stirs up conflict,
but one slow to anger calms strife.

Proverbs 15:18

When a person's ways please the LORD,
he makes even his enemies to be at peace with him.

Proverbs 16:7

A contrary person spreads conflict,
and a gossip separates close friends.

Proverbs 16:28

Better a dry crust with peace
than a house full of feasting with strife.

Proverbs 17:1

Whoever conceals an offense promotes love,
but whoever gossips about it separates friends.

Proverbs 17:9

To start a conflict is to release a flood;
stop the dispute before it breaks out.

Proverbs 17:14

One who loves to offend loves strife;
one who builds a high threshold invites injury.

Proverbs 17:19

When a wicked person comes, contempt also comes,
and along with dishonor, derision.

Proverbs 18:3

Casting the lot ends quarrels
and separates powerful opponents.

Proverbs 18:18

An offended brother is harder to reach
than a fortified city,
and quarrels are like the bars of a fortress.

Proverbs 18:19

Honor belongs to the person who ends a dispute,
but any fool can get himself into a quarrel.

Proverbs 20:3

A secret gift soothes anger,
and a covert bribe, fierce rage.

Proverbs 21:14

Drive out a mocker, and conflict goes too;
then quarreling and dishonor will cease.

Proverbs 22:10

Singing songs to a troubled heart
is like taking off clothing on a cold day
or like pouring vinegar on soda.

Proverbs 25:20

The north wind produces rain,
and a backbiting tongue, angry looks.

Proverbs 25:23

A person who is passing by and meddles in a quarrel
that's not his
is like one who grabs a dog by the ears.

Like a madman who throws flaming darts and deadly
arrows,
so is the person who deceives his neighbor
and says, "I was only joking!"

Proverbs 26:17-19

Without wood, fire goes out;
without a gossip, conflict dies down.
As charcoal for embers and wood for fire,
so is a quarrelsome person for kindling strife.

Proverbs 26:20-21

A greedy person stirs up conflict,
but whoever trusts in the LORD will prosper.

Proverbs 28:25

Mockers inflame a city,
but the wise turn away anger.

Proverbs 29:8

If a wise person goes to court with a fool,
there will be ranting and raving but no resolution.

Proverbs 29:9

An angry person stirs up conflict,
and a hot-tempered one increases rebellion.

Proverbs 29:22

If you have been foolish by exalting yourself
or if you've been scheming,
put your hand over your mouth.
For the churning of milk produces butter,
and twisting a nose draws blood,
and stirring up anger produces strife.

Proverbs 30:32-33

Deception

Though the lips of the forbidden woman drip honey
and her words are smoother than oil,
in the end she's as bitter as wormwood
and as sharp as a double-edged sword.
Her feet go down to death;
her steps head straight for Sheol.
She doesn't consider the path of life;
she doesn't know that her ways are unstable.

Proverbs 5:3-6

She seduces him with her persistent pleading;
she lures with her flattering talk.
He follows her impulsively
like an ox going to the slaughter,
like a deer bounding toward a trap
until an arrow pierces its liver,
like a bird darting into a snare—
he doesn't know it will cost him his life.

Proverbs 7:21-23

The thoughts of the righteous are just,
but guidance from the wicked is deceitful.

Proverbs 12:5

Whoever speaks the truth declares what is right,
but a false witness speaks deceit.

Proverbs 12:17

One person pretends to be rich but has nothing;
another pretends to be poor but has abundant wealth.

Proverbs 13:7

The sensible person's wisdom is to consider his way,
but the stupidity of fools deceives them.

Proverbs 14:8

There is a way that seems right to a person,
but its end is the way to death.

Proverbs 14:12, 16:25

The one who narrows his eyes is planning deceptions;
the one who compresses his lips brings about evil.

Proverbs 16:30

A bribe seems like a magic stone to its owner;
wherever he turns, he succeeds.

Proverbs 17:8

The wealth of the rich is his fortified city;
in his imagination it is like a high wall.

Proverbs 18:11

The first to state his case seems right
until another comes and cross-examines him.

Proverbs 18:17

"It's worthless, it's worthless!" the buyer says,
but after he is on his way, he gloats.

Proverbs 20:14

Food gained by fraud is sweet to a person,
but afterward his mouth is full of gravel.

Proverbs 20:17

Making a fortune through a lying tongue
is a vanishing mist, a pursuit of death.

Proverbs 21:6

The mouth of the forbidden woman is a deep pit;
a man cursed by the LORD will fall into it.

Proverbs 22:14

When you sit down to dine with a ruler,
consider carefully what is before you,
and put a knife to your throat
if you have a big appetite;
don't desire his choice food,
for that food is deceptive.

Proverbs 23:1-3

Don't wear yourself out to get rich;
because you know better, stop!
As soon as your eyes fly to it, it disappears,
for it makes wings for itself
and flies like an eagle to the sky.

Proverbs 23:4-5

Don't eat a stingy person's bread,
and don't desire his choice food,
for it's like someone calculating inwardly.
"Eat and drink," he says to you,
but his heart is not with you.
You will vomit the little you've eaten
and waste your pleasant words.

Proverbs 23:6-8

My son, give me your heart,
and let your eyes observe my ways.
For a prostitute is a deep pit,
and a wayward woman is a narrow well;
indeed, she sets an ambush like a robber
and increases the number of unfaithful people.

Proverbs 23:26-28

Don't gaze at wine because it is red,
because it gleams in the cup

and goes down smoothly.
In the end it bites like a snake
and stings like a viper.

Proverbs 23:31-32

The one who boasts about a gift that does not exist
is like clouds and wind without rain.

Proverbs 25:14

Smooth lips with an evil heart
are like glaze on an earthen vessel.

Proverbs 26:23

Like a madman who throws flaming darts and deadly
arrows,
so is the person who deceives his neighbor
and says, "I was only joking!"

Proverbs 26:18-19

A hateful person disguises himself with his speech
and harbors deceit within.
When he speaks graciously, don't believe him,
for there are seven detestable things in his heart.
Though his hatred is concealed by deception,
his evil will be revealed in the assembly.

Proverbs 26:24-26

Better an open reprimand
than concealed love.

Proverbs 27:5

The wounds of a friend are trustworthy,
but the kisses of an enemy are excessive.

Proverbs 27:6

Sheol and Abaddon are never satisfied,
and people's eyes are never satisfied.

Proverbs 27:20

Charm is deceptive and beauty is fleeting,
but a woman who fears the LORD will be praised.

Proverbs 31:30

Diligence

Idle hands make one poor,
but diligent hands bring riches.

Proverbs 10:4

The son who gathers during summer is prudent;
the son who sleeps during harvest is disgraceful.

Proverbs 10:5

The one who works his land will have plenty of food,
but whoever chases fantasies lacks sense.

Proverbs 12:11

The wicked desire what evil people have caught,
but the root of the righteous is productive.

Proverbs 12:12

A person will be satisfied with good
by the fruit of his mouth,
and the work of a person's hands will reward him.

Proverbs 12:14

The diligent hand will rule,
but laziness will lead to forced labor.

Proverbs 12:24

A lazy hunter doesn't roast his game,
but to a diligent person, his wealth is precious.

Proverbs 12:27

The slacker craves, yet has nothing,
but the diligent is fully satisfied.

Proverbs 13:4

Wealth obtained by fraud will dwindle,
but whoever earns it through labor will multiply it.

Proverbs 13:11

Where there are no oxen, the feeding trough is empty,
but an abundant harvest comes through the strength of
an ox.

Proverbs 14:4

There is profit in all hard work,
but endless talk leads only to poverty.

Proverbs 14:23

A worker's appetite works for him
because his hunger urges him on.

Proverbs 16:26

A person's gift opens doors for him
and brings him before the great.

Proverbs 18:16

The plans of the diligent certainly lead to profit,
but anyone who is reckless certainly becomes poor.

Proverbs 21:5

Do you see a person skilled in his work?
He will stand in the presence of kings.
He will not stand in the presence of the unknown.

Proverbs 22:29

Complete your outdoor work, and prepare your field;
afterward, build your house.

Proverbs 24:27

Whoever tends a fig tree will eat its fruit,
and whoever looks after his master will be honored.

Proverbs 27:18

The one who works his land
will have plenty of food,
but whoever chases fantasies
will have his fill of poverty.

Proverbs 28:19

She selects wool and flax
and works with willing hands.
She is like the merchant ships,
bringing her food from far away.
She rises while it is still night
and provides food for her household
and portions for her female servants.
She evaluates a field and buys it;
she plants a vineyard with her earnings.
She draws on her strength
and reveals that her arms are strong.
She sees that her profits are good,
and her lamp never goes out at night.
She extends her hands to the spinning staff,
and her hands hold the spindle.
She is not afraid for her household when it snows,
for all in her household are doubly clothed.
She makes her own bed coverings;
her clothing is fine linen and purple.
She watches over the activities of her household
and is never idle.

Proverbs 31:13-19,21-22,27

Discernment

The proverbs of Solomon son of David, king of Israel:
For learning wisdom and discipline;
for understanding insightful sayings;
for receiving prudent instruction
in righteousness, justice, and integrity;
for teaching shrewdness to the inexperienced,
knowledge and discretion to a young man—
let a wise person listen and increase learning,
and let a discerning person obtain guidance—
for understanding a proverb or a parable,
the words of the wise, and their riddles.

Proverbs 1:1-6

Discretion will watch over you,
and understanding will guard you.

Proverbs 2:11

My son, pay attention to my wisdom;
listen closely to my understanding
so that you may maintain discretion
and your lips safeguard knowledge.

Proverbs 5:1-2

I, wisdom, share a home with shrewdness
and have knowledge and discretion.

Proverbs 8:12

Wisdom resides in the heart of the discerning;
she is known even among fools.

Proverbs 14:33

The one who understands a matter finds success,
and the one who trusts in the LORD will be happy.

Proverbs 16:20

Anyone with a wise heart is called discerning,
and pleasant speech increases learning.

Proverbs 16:21

Even a fool is considered wise when he keeps silent—
discerning, when he seals his lips.

Proverbs 17:28

The mind of the discerning acquires knowledge,
and the ear of the wise seeks it.

Proverbs 18:15

Strike a mocker, and the inexperienced learn a lesson;
rebuke the discerning, and he gains knowledge.

Proverbs 19:25

Counsel in a person's heart is deep water;
but a person of understanding draws it out.

Proverbs 20:5

A king sitting on a throne to judge
separates out all evil with his eyes.

Proverbs 20:8

The hearing ear and the seeing eye—
the LORD made them both.

Proverbs 20:12

When a land is in rebellion, it has many rulers,
but with a discerning and knowledgeable person, it endures.

Proverbs 28:2

The evil do not understand justice,
but those who seek the LORD understand everything.

Proverbs 28:5

A rich person is wise in his own eyes,
but a poor one who has discernment sees through him.

Proverbs 28:11

Discipline

The fear of the LORD
is the beginning of knowledge;
fools despise wisdom and discipline.

Proverbs 1:7

Do not despise the LORD's instruction, my son,
and do not loathe his discipline;
for the LORD disciplines the one he loves,
just as a father disciplines the son in whom he delights.

Proverbs 3:11-12

At the end of your life, you will lament
when your physical body has been consumed,
and you will say, "How I hated discipline,
and how my heart despised correction.
I didn't obey my teachers

or listen closely to my instructors.
I am on the verge of complete ruin
before the entire community."

Proverbs 5:11-14

A wicked man's iniquities will trap him;
he will become tangled in the ropes of his own sin.
He will die because there is no discipline,
and be lost because of his great stupidity.

Proverbs 5:22-23

For a command is a lamp, teaching is a light,
and corrective discipline is the way to life.
They will protect you from an evil woman,
from the flattering tongue of a wayward woman.

Proverbs 6:23-24

Wisdom is found on the lips of the discerning,
but a rod is for the back of the one who lacks sense.

Proverbs 10:13

A wise son responds to his father's discipline,
but a mocker doesn't listen to rebuke.

Proverbs 13:1

Poverty and disgrace come to those
who ignore discipline,
but the one who accepts correction will be honored.

Proverbs 13:18

The one who will not use the rod hates his son,
but the one who loves him disciplines him diligently.

Proverbs 13:24

A fool despises his father's discipline,
but a person who accepts correction is sensible.

Proverbs 15:5

Discipline is harsh for the one who leaves the path;
the one who hates correction will die.

Proverbs 15:10

Anyone who ignores discipline despises himself,
but whoever listens to correction acquires good sense.

Proverbs 15:32

Discipline your son while there is hope;
don't set your heart on being the cause of his death.

Proverbs 19:18

Lashes and wounds purge away evil,
and beatings cleanse the innermost parts.

Proverbs 20:30

Start a youth out on his way;
even when he grows old he will not depart from it.

Proverbs 22:6

Foolishness is bound to the heart of a youth;
a rod of discipline will separate it from him.

Proverbs 22:15

Apply yourself to discipline
and listen to words of knowledge.

Proverbs 23:12

Don't withhold discipline from a youth;
if you punish him with a rod, he will not die.
Punish him with a rod,
and you will rescue his life from Sheol.

Proverbs 23:13-14

A rod of correction imparts wisdom,
but a youth left to himself
is a disgrace to his mother.

Proverbs 29:15

Discipline your child, and it will bring you peace of mind
and give you delight.

Proverbs 29:17

A servant cannot be disciplined by words;
though he understands, he doesn't respond.

Proverbs 29:19

Drunkenness

Wine is a mocker, beer is a brawler;
whoever goes astray because of them is not wise.

Proverbs 20:1

The one who loves pleasure will become poor;
whoever loves wine and oil will not get rich.

Proverbs 21:17

Listen, my son, and be wise;
keep your mind on the right course.
Don't associate with those who drink too much wine
or with those who gorge themselves on meat.
For the drunkard and the glutton will become poor,
and grogginess will clothe them in rags.

Proverbs 23:19-21

Who has woe? Who has sorrow?
Who has conflicts? Who has complaints?
Who has wounds for no reason?
Who has red eyes?

Those who linger over wine;
those who go looking for mixed wine.
Don't gaze at wine because it is red,
because it gleams in the cup
and goes down smoothly.
In the end it bites like a snake
and stings like a viper.
Your eyes will see strange things,
and you will say absurd things.
You'll be like someone sleeping out at sea
or lying down on the top of a ship's mast.
"They struck me, but I feel no pain!
They beat me, but I didn't know it!
When will I wake up?
I'll look for another drink."

Proverbs 23:29-35

It is not for kings, Lemuel,
it is not for kings to drink wine
or for rulers to desire beer.
Otherwise, he will drink,
forget what is decreed,
and pervert justice for all the oppressed.
Give beer to one who is dying
and wine to one whose life is bitter.
Let him drink so that he can forget his poverty
and remember his trouble no more.

Proverbs 31:4-7

Excess

When you sit down to dine with a ruler,
consider carefully what is before you,
and put a knife to your throat
if you have a big appetite;
don't desire his choice food,
for that food is deceptive.

Proverbs 23:1-3

Listen, my son, and be wise;
keep your mind on the right course.
Don't associate with those who drink too much wine
or with those who gorge themselves on meat.
For the drunkard and the glutton will become poor,
and grogginess will clothe them in rags.

Proverbs 23:19-21

If you find honey, eat only what you need;
otherwise, you'll get sick from it and vomit.

Proverbs 25:16

It is not good to eat too much honey
or to seek glory after glory.

Proverbs 25:27

A person who is full tramples on a honeycomb,
but to a hungry person, any bitter thing is sweet.

Proverbs 27:7

A discerning son keeps the law,
but a companion of gluttons humiliates his father.

Proverbs 28:7

Faithfulness

He is a shield for those who live with integrity
so that he may guard the paths of justice
and protect the way of his faithful followers.

Proverbs 2:7b-8

Never let loyalty and faithfulness leave you.
Tie them around your neck;
write them on the tablet of your heart.

Proverbs 3:3

Honor the LORD with your possessions
and with the first produce of your entire harvest;
then your barns will be completely filled,
and your vats will overflow with new wine.

Proverbs 3:9-10

Lying lips are detestable to the LORD,
but faithful people are his delight.

Proverbs 12:22

Don't those who plan evil go astray?
But those who plan good find loyalty and faithfulness.

Proverbs 14:22

Iniquity is atoned for by loyalty and faithfulness,
and one turns from evil by the fear of the LORD.

Proverbs 16:6

Many a person proclaims his own loyalty,
but who can find a trustworthy person?

Proverbs 20:6

Loyalty and faithfulness guard a king;
through loyalty he maintains his throne.

Proverbs 20:28

A faithful person will have many blessings,
but one in a hurry to get rich
will not go unpunished.

Proverbs 28:20

Favor

Listen, my son, to your father's instruction,
and don't reject your mother's teaching,
for they will be a garland of favor on your head
and pendants around your neck.

Proverbs 1:8-9

Never let loyalty and faithfulness leave you.
Tie them around your neck;
write them on the tablet of your heart.
Then you will find favor and high regard
with God and people.

Proverbs 3:3-4

She [Understanding] will place a garland of favor on
your head;
she will give you a crown of beauty.

Proverbs 4:9

For the one who finds me [Wisdom] finds life
and obtains favor from the LORD,
but the one who misses me harms himself;
all who hate me love death.

Proverbs 8:35-36

Blessings are on the head of the righteous,
but the mouth of the wicked conceals violence.

Proverbs 10:6

The remembrance of the righteous is a blessing,
but the name of the wicked will rot.

Proverbs 10:7

The LORD's blessing enriches,
and he adds no painful effort to it.

Proverbs 10:22

The one who searches for what is good seeks favor,
but if someone looks for trouble, it will come to him.

Proverbs 11:27

One who is good obtains favor from the LORD,
but he condemns a person who schemes.

Proverbs 12:2

Good sense wins favor,
but the way of the treacherous never changes.

Proverbs 13:15

Disaster pursues sinners,
but good rewards the righteous.

Proverbs 13:21

A man who finds a wife finds a good thing
and obtains favor from the LORD.

Proverbs 18:22

Many seek a ruler's favor,
and everyone is a friend of one who gives gifts.

Proverbs 19:6

A good name is to be chosen over great wealth;
favor is better than silver and gold.

Proverbs 22:1

These sayings also belong to the wise:
It is not good to show partiality in judgment.

Whoever says to the guilty, "You are innocent"—
peoples will curse him, and nations will denounce him;
but it will go well with those who convict the guilty,
and a generous blessing will come to them.

Proverbs 24:23-25

A faithful person will have many blessings,
but one in a hurry to get rich
will not go unpunished.

Proverbs 28:20

One who rebukes a person will later find more favor
than one who flatters with his tongue.

Proverbs 28:23

Fear of the LORD

The fear of the LORD
is the beginning of knowledge;
fools despise wisdom and discipline.

Proverbs 1:7

Because they hated knowledge,
didn't choose to fear the LORD,

were not interested in my counsel,
and rejected all my correction,
they will eat the fruit of their way
and be glutted with their own schemes.

Proverbs 1:29-31

My son, if you accept my words
and store up my commands within you,
listening closely to wisdom
and directing your heart to understanding;
furthermore, if you call out to insight
and lift your voice to understanding,
if you seek it like silver
and search for it like hidden treasure,
then you will understand the fear of the LORD
and discover the knowledge of God.

Proverbs 2:1-5

Don't be wise in your own eyes;
fear the LORD and turn away from evil.

Proverbs 3:7

To fear the LORD is to hate evil.

Proverbs 8:13a

The fear of the LORD is the beginning of wisdom,
and the knowledge of the Holy One is understanding.

Proverbs 9:10

The fear of the LORD prolongs life,
but the years of the wicked are cut short.

Proverbs 10:27

Whoever lives with integrity fears the LORD,
but the one who is devious in his ways despises him.

Proverbs 14:2

In the fear of the LORD one has strong confidence
and his children have a refuge.

Proverbs 14:26

The fear of the LORD is a fountain of life,
turning people away from the snares of death.

Proverbs 14:27

Better a little with the fear of the LORD
than great treasure with turmoil.

Proverbs 15:16

The fear of the LORD is what wisdom teaches,
and humility comes before honor.

Proverbs 15:33

Iniquity is atoned for by loyalty and faithfulness,
and one turns from evil by the fear of the LORD.

Proverbs 16:6

The fear of the LORD leads to life;
one will sleep at night without danger.

Proverbs 19:23

Humility, the fear of the LORD,
results in wealth, honor, and life.

Proverbs 22:4

Don't let your heart envy sinners;
instead, always fear the LORD.
For then you will have a future,
and your hope will not be dashed.

Proverbs 23:17-18

My son, fear the LORD, as well as the king,
and don't associate with rebels,
for destruction will come suddenly from them;
who knows what distress these two can bring?

Proverbs 24:21-22

The fear of mankind is a snare,
but the one who trusts in the LORD is protected.

Proverbs 29:25

Charm is deceptive and beauty is fleeting,
but a woman who fears the LORD will be praised.

Proverbs 31:30

Fidelity

Drink water from your own cistern,
water flowing from your own well.
Should your springs flow in the streets,
streams in the public squares?
They should be for you alone
and not for you to share with strangers.
Let your fountain be blessed,
and take pleasure in the wife of your youth.
A loving deer, a graceful doe—
let her breasts always satisfy you;
be lost in her love forever.
Why, my son, would you lose yourself
with a forbidden woman
or embrace a wayward woman?

Proverbs 5:15-20

Don't lust in your heart for her beauty
or let her captivate you with her eyelashes.
For a prostitute's fee is only a loaf of bread,

but the wife of another man goes after a precious life.
Can a man embrace fire
and his clothes not be burned?
Can a man walk on burning coals
without scorching his feet?
So it is with the one who sleeps with
another man's wife;
no one who touches her will go unpunished.
People don't despise the thief if he steals
to satisfy himself when he is hungry.
Still, if caught, he must pay seven times as much;
he must give up all the wealth in his house.
The one who commits adultery lacks sense;
whoever does so destroys himself.
He will get a beating and dishonor,
and his disgrace will never be removed.
For jealousy enrages a husband,
and he will show no mercy when he takes revenge.
He will not be appeased by anything
or be persuaded by lavish bribes.

Proverbs 6:25-35

Don't let your heart turn aside to her ways;
don't stray onto her paths.
For she has brought many down to death;
her victims are countless.
Her house is the road to Sheol,
descending to the chambers of death.

Proverbs 7:25-27

What is desirable in a person is his fidelity;
better to be a poor person than a liar.

Proverbs 19:22

The mouth of the forbidden woman is a deep pit;
a man cursed by the LORD will fall into it.

Proverbs 22:14

My son, give me your heart,
and let your eyes observe my ways.
For a prostitute is a deep pit,
and a wayward woman is a narrow well;
indeed, she sets an ambush like a robber
and increases the number of unfaithful people.

Proverbs 23:26-28

Folly

Then they will call me [Wisdom], but I won't answer;
they will search for me, but won't find me.
Because they hated knowledge,
didn't choose to fear the LORD,
were not interested in my counsel,
and rejected all my correction,
they will eat the fruit of their way
and be glutted with their own schemes.
For the apostasy of the inexperienced will kill them,
and the complacency of fools will destroy them.
But whoever listens to me will live securely
and be undisturbed by the dread of danger.

Proverbs 1:28-33

It [Wisdom] will rescue you from the way of evil—
from anyone who says perverse things,
from those who abandon the right paths
to walk in ways of darkness,
from those who enjoy doing evil
and celebrate perversion,
whose paths are crooked,
and whose ways are devious.
It will rescue you from a forbidden woman,
from a wayward woman with her flattering talk,
who abandons the companion of her youth
and forgets the covenant of her God;
for her house sinks down to death
and her ways to the land of the departed spirits.
None return who go to her;
none reach the paths of life.
So follow the way of the good,
and keep to the paths of the righteous.

Proverbs 2:12-20

The wise will inherit honor,
but he holds up fools to dishonor.

Proverbs 3:35

The one who corrects a mocker
will bring abuse on himself;
the one who rebukes the wicked will get hurt.

Proverbs 9:7

Folly is a rowdy woman;
she is gullible and knows nothing.
She sits by the doorway of her house,
on a seat at the highest point of the city,
calling to those who pass by,
who go straight ahead on their paths:
"Whoever is inexperienced, enter here!"
To the one who lacks sense, she says,

"Stolen water is sweet,
and bread eaten secretly is tasty!"
But he doesn't know that the departed spirits are there,
that her guests are in the depths of Sheol.

Proverbs 9:13-18

As shameful conduct is pleasure for a fool,
so wisdom is for a person of understanding.

Proverbs 10:23

The one who brings ruin on his household
will inherit the wind,
and a fool will be a slave
to someone whose heart is wise.

Proverbs 11:29

Desire fulfilled is sweet to the taste,
but to turn from evil is detestable to fools.

Proverbs 13:19

The one who walks with the wise will become wise,
but a companion of fools will suffer harm.

Proverbs 13:20

Every wise woman builds her house,
but a foolish one tears it down with her own hands.

Proverbs 14:1

The sensible person's wisdom is to consider his way,
but the stupidity of fools deceives them.

Proverbs 14:8

There is a way that seems right to a person,
but its end is the way to death.

Proverbs 14:12

The crown of the wise is their wealth,
but the foolishness of fools produces foolishness.

Proverbs 14:24

A wise son brings joy to his father,
but a foolish man despises his mother.

Proverbs 15:20

Insight is a fountain of life for its possessor,
but the discipline of fools is folly.

Proverbs 16:22

There is a way that seems right to a person,
but its end is the way to death.

Proverbs 16:25

Eloquent words are not appropriate on a fool's lips;
how much worse are lies for a ruler.

Proverbs 17:7

Better for a person to meet a bear robbed of her cubs
than a fool in his foolishness.

Proverbs 17:12

Why does a fool have money in his hand
with no intention of buying wisdom?

Proverbs 17:16

A man fathers a fool to his own sorrow;
the father of a fool has no joy.

Proverbs 17:21

Wisdom is the focus of the perceptive,
but a fool's eyes roam to the ends of the earth.

Proverbs 17:24

A foolish son is grief to his father
and bitterness to the one who bore him.

Proverbs 17:25

A person's own foolishness leads him astray,
yet his heart rages against the LORD.

Proverbs 19:3

Judgments are prepared for mockers,
and beatings for the backs of fools.

Proverbs 19:29

Precious treasure and oil are in the dwelling of a wise
person,
but a fool consumes them.

Proverbs 21:20

Don't speak to a fool,
for he will despise the insight of your words.

Proverbs 23:9

Wisdom is inaccessible to a fool;
he does not open his mouth at the city gate.

Proverbs 24:7

The one who plots evil
will be called a schemer.
A foolish scheme is sin,
and a mocker is detestable to people.

Proverbs 24:8-9

Like snow in summer and rain at harvest,
honor is inappropriate for a fool.

Proverbs 26:1

A whip for the horse, a bridle for the donkey,
and a rod for the backs of fools.
Don't answer a fool according to his foolishness
or you'll be like him yourself.
Answer a fool according to his foolishness
or he'll become wise in his own eyes.
The one who sends a message by a fool's hand
cuts off his own feet and drinks violence.
A proverb in the mouth of a fool
is like lame legs that hang limp.
Giving honor to a fool
is like binding a stone in a sling.
A proverb in the mouth of a fool
is like a stick with thorns,

brandished by the hand of a drunkard.
The one who hires a fool or who hires those passing by
is like an archer who wounds everyone.
As a dog returns to its vomit,
so also a fool repeats his foolishness.
Do you see a person who is wise in his own eyes?
There is more hope for a fool than for him.

Proverbs 26:3-12

A stone is heavy and sand, a burden,
but aggravation from a fool outweighs them both.

Proverbs 27:3

Anyone wandering from his home
is like a bird wandering from its nest.

Proverbs 27:8

Though you grind a fool
in a mortar with a pestle along with grain,
you will not separate his foolishness from him.

Proverbs 27:22

The one who trusts in himself is a fool,
but one who walks in wisdom will be safe.

Proverbs 28:26

A man who loves wisdom brings joy to his father,
but one who consorts with prostitutes destroys his wealth.

Proverbs 29:3

If a wise person goes to court with a fool,
there will be ranting and raving but no resolution.

Proverbs 29:9

The words of Agur son of Jakeh. The pronouncement.
The man's oration to Ithiel, to Ithiel and Ucal:
I am more stupid than any other person,
and I lack a human's ability to understand.
I have not gained wisdom,
and I have no knowledge of the Holy One.

Who has gone up to heaven and come down?
Who has gathered the wind in his hands?
Who has bound up the waters in a cloak?
Who has established all the ends of the earth?
What is his name,
and what is the name of his son—
if you know?

Proverbs 30:1-4

Friendship

Don't envy a violent man
or choose any of his ways;
for the devious are detestable to the LORD,
but he is a friend to the upright.

Proverbs 3:31-32

A contrary person spreads conflict,
and a gossip separates close friends.

Proverbs 16:28

Whoever conceals an offense promotes love,
but whoever gossips about it separates friends.

Proverbs 17:9

A friend loves at all times,
and a brother is born for a difficult time.

Proverbs 17:17

One without sense enters an agreement
and puts up security for his friend.

Proverbs 17:18

One who isolates himself pursues selfish desires;
he rebels against all sound wisdom.

Proverbs 18:1

One with many friends may be harmed,
but there is a friend who stays closer than a brother.

Proverbs 18:24

Wealth attracts many friends,
but a poor person is separated from his friend.

Proverbs 19:4

Many seek a ruler's favor,
and everyone is a friend of one who gives gifts.

Proverbs 19:6

All the brothers of a poor person hate him;
how much more do his friends
keep their distance from him!
He may pursue them with words,
but they are not there.

Proverbs 19:7

The one who loves a pure heart
and gracious lips—the king is his friend.

Proverbs 22:11

The wounds of a friend are trustworthy,
but the kisses of an enemy are excessive.

Proverbs 27:6

Oil and incense bring joy to the heart,
and the sweetness of a friend is better than self-counsel.

Proverbs 27:9

Don't abandon your friend or your father's friend,
and don't go to your brother's house
in your time of calamity;
better a neighbor nearby than a brother far away.

Proverbs 27:10

Iron sharpens iron,
and one person sharpens another.

Proverbs 27:17

Greed

When the wicked person dies,
his expectation comes to nothing,
and hope placed in wealth vanishes.

Proverbs 11:7

One person gives freely,
yet gains more;
another withholds what is right,
only to become poor.

Proverbs 11:24

People will curse anyone who hoards grain,
but a blessing will come to the one who sells it.

Proverbs 11:26

Anyone trusting in his riches will fall,
but the righteous will flourish like foliage.

Proverbs 11:28

Wealth obtained by fraud will dwindle,
but whoever earns it through labor will multiply it.

Proverbs 13:11

An inheritance gained prematurely
will not be blessed ultimately.

Proverbs 20:21

Don't wear yourself out to get rich;
because you know better, stop!
As soon as your eyes fly to it, it disappears,
for it makes wings for itself
and flies like an eagle to the sky.

Proverbs 23:4-5

Whoever increases his wealth through excessive interest
collects it for one who is kind to the poor.

Proverbs 28:8

A faithful person will have many blessings,
but one in a hurry to get rich
will not go unpunished.

Proverbs 28:20

A greedy one is in a hurry for wealth;
he doesn't know that poverty will come to him.

Proverbs 28:22

A greedy person stirs up conflict,
but whoever trusts in the LORD will prosper.

Proverbs 28:25

Guidance

Listen, my son, to your father's instruction,
and don't reject your mother's teaching,
for they will be a garland of favor on your head
and pendants around your neck.

Proverbs 1:8-9

Do not despise the LORD's instruction, my son,
and do not loathe his discipline;
for the LORD disciplines the one he loves,
just as a father disciplines the son in whom he delights.

Proverbs 3:11-12

At the end of your life, you will lament
when your physical body has been consumed,
and you will say, "How I hated discipline,
and how my heart despised correction.
I didn't obey my teachers
or listen closely to my instructors.
I am on the verge of complete ruin
before the entire community."

Proverbs 5:11-14

A wicked man's iniquities will trap him;
he will become tangled in the ropes of his own sin.

He will die because there is no discipline,
and be lost because of his great stupidity.

Proverbs 5:22-23

For a command is a lamp, teaching is a light,
and corrective discipline is the way to life.
They will protect you from an evil woman,
from the flattering tongue of a wayward woman.

Proverbs 6:23-24

Keep my commands and live,
and guard my instructions
as you would the pupil of your eye.

Proverbs 7:2

Accept my instruction instead of silver,
and knowledge rather than pure gold.

Proverbs 8:10

Listen to instruction and be wise;
don't ignore it.

Proverbs 8:33

The one who corrects a mocker
will bring abuse on himself;
the one who rebukes the wicked will get hurt.
Don't rebuke a mocker, or he will hate you;
rebuke the wise, and he will love you.
Instruct the wise, and he will be wiser still;
teach the righteous, and he will learn more.

Proverbs 9:7-9

A wise heart accepts commands,
but foolish lips will be destroyed.

Proverbs 10:8

The one who follows instruction is on the path to life,
but the one who rejects correction goes astray.

Proverbs 10:17

Without guidance, a people will fall,
but with many counselors there is deliverance.

Proverbs 11:14

Whoever loves discipline loves knowledge,
but one who hates correction is stupid.

Proverbs 12:1

A fool's way is right in his own eyes,
but whoever listens to counsel is wise.

Proverbs 12:15

A wise son responds to his father's discipline,
but a mocker doesn't listen to rebuke.

Proverbs 13:1

Arrogance leads to nothing but strife,
but wisdom is gained by those who take advice.

Proverbs 13:10

The one who has contempt for instruction will pay the
penalty,
but the one who respects a command will be rewarded.

Proverbs 13:13

A wise person's instruction is a fountain of life,
turning people away from the snares of death.

Proverbs 13:14

Poverty and disgrace come to those
who ignore discipline,
but the one who accepts correction will be honored.

Proverbs 13:18

A fool despises his father's discipline,
but a person who accepts correction is sensible.

Proverbs 15:5

Discipline is harsh for the one who leaves the path;
the one who hates correction will die.

Proverbs 15:10

A mocker doesn't love one who corrects him;
he will not consult the wise.

Proverbs 15:12

Plans fail when there is no counsel,
but with many advisers they succeed.

Proverbs 15:22

One who listens to life-giving rebukes
will be at home among the wise.

Proverbs 15:31

Anyone who ignores discipline despises himself,
but whoever listens to correction acquires good sense.

Proverbs 15:32

A rebuke cuts into a perceptive person
more than a hundred lashes into a fool.

Proverbs 17:10

One who isolates himself pursues selfish desires;
he rebels against all sound wisdom.

Proverbs 18:1

The one who keeps commands preserves himself;
one who disregards his ways will die.

Proverbs 19:16

Listen to counsel and receive instruction
so that you may be wise later in life.

Proverbs 19:20

Strike a mocker, and the inexperienced learn a lesson;
rebuke the discerning, and he gains knowledge.

Proverbs 19:25

If you stop listening to correction, my son,
you will stray from the words of knowledge.

Proverbs 19:27

Counsel in a person's heart is deep water;
but a person of understanding draws it out.

Proverbs 20:5

Finalize plans with counsel,
and wage war with sound guidance.

Proverbs 20:18

When a mocker is punished,
the inexperienced become wiser;
when one teaches a wise man,
he acquires knowledge.

Proverbs 21:11

Apply yourself to discipline
and listen to words of knowledge.

Proverbs 23:12

Buy—and do not sell—truth,
wisdom, instruction, and understanding.

Proverbs 23:23

A wise warrior is better than a strong one,
and a man of knowledge than one of strength;
for you should wage war with sound guidance—
victory comes with many counselors.

Proverbs 24:5-6

A word spoken at the right time
is like gold apples in silver settings.
A wise correction to a receptive ear
is like a gold ring or an ornament of gold.

Proverbs 25:11-12

Better an open reprimand
than concealed love.

Proverbs 27:5

Iron sharpens iron,
and one person sharpens another.

Proverbs 27:17

One who rebukes a person will later find more favor
than one who flatters with his tongue.

Proverbs 28:23

One who becomes stiff-necked,
after many reprimands
will be shattered instantly—
beyond recovery.

Proverbs 29:1

Without revelation people run wild,
but one who follows divine instruction will be happy.

Proverbs 29:18

Happiness

Happy is a man who finds wisdom
and who acquires understanding,
for she is more profitable than silver,
and her revenue is better than gold.
She is more precious than jewels;
nothing you desire can equal her.

Proverbs 3:13-15

She [Wisdom] is a tree of life to those who embrace her,
and those who hold on to her are happy.

Proverbs 3:18

And now, sons, listen to me [Wisdom];
those who keep my ways are happy.

Proverbs 8:32

Anyone who listens to me is happy,
watching at my doors every day,
waiting by the posts of my doorway.

Proverbs 8:34

A wise son brings joy to his father,
but a foolish son, heartache to his mother.

Proverbs 10:1

The hope of the righteous is joy,
but the expectation of the wicked will perish.

Proverbs 10:28

Deceit is in the hearts of those who plot evil,
but those who promote peace have joy.

Proverbs 12:20

Anxiety in a person's heart weighs it down,
but a good word cheers it up.

Proverbs 12:25

Even in laughter a heart may be sad,
and joy may end in grief.

Proverbs 14:13

The one who despises his neighbor sins,
but whoever shows kindness to the poor will be happy.

Proverbs 14:21

A joyful heart makes a face cheerful,
but a sad heart produces a broken spirit.

Proverbs 15:13

All the days of the oppressed are miserable,
but a cheerful heart has a continual feast.

Proverbs 15:15

Bright eyes cheer the heart;
good news strengthens the bones.

Proverbs 15:30

The one who understands a matter finds success,
and the one who trusts in the LORD will be happy.

Proverbs 16:20

A joyful heart is good medicine,
but a broken spirit dries up the bones.

Proverbs 17:22

A person's spirit can endure sickness,
but who can survive a broken spirit?

Proverbs 18:14

A righteous person acts with integrity;
his children who come after him will be happy.

Proverbs 20:7

The father of a righteous son will rejoice greatly,
and one who fathers a wise son will delight in him.
Let your father and mother have joy,
and let her who gave birth to you rejoice.

Proverbs 23:24-25

Be wise, my son, and bring my heart joy,
so that I can answer anyone who taunts me.

Proverbs 27:11

Happy is the one who is always reverent,
but one who hardens his heart falls into trouble.

Proverbs 28:14

Without revelation people run wild,
but one who follows divine instruction will be happy.

Proverbs 29:18

The Heart

For wisdom will enter your heart,
and knowledge will delight you.

Proverbs 2:10

Never let loyalty and faithfulness leave you.
Tie them around your neck;
write them on the tablet of your heart.

Proverbs 3:3

Trust in the LORD with all your heart,
and do not rely on your own understanding.

Proverbs 3:5

When I was a son with my father,
tender and precious to my mother,
he taught me and said:
"Your heart must hold on to my words.
Keep my commands and live."

Proverbs 4:3-4

My son, pay attention to my words;
listen closely to my sayings.
Don't lose sight of them;
keep them within your heart.

Proverbs 4:20-21

Guard your heart above all else,
for it is the source of life.

Proverbs 4:23

He always plots evil with perversity in his heart;
he stirs up trouble.

Proverbs 6:14

My son, keep your father's command,
and don't reject your mother's teaching.
Always bind them to your heart;
tie them around your neck.

Proverbs 6:20-21

Don't lust in your heart for her beauty
or let her captivate you with her eyelashes.

Proverbs 6:25

Keep my commands and live,
and guard my instructions
as you would the pupil of your eye.
Tie them to your fingers;
write them on the tablet of your heart.

Proverbs 7:2-3

Don't let your heart turn aside to her ways;
don't stray onto her paths.

Proverbs 7:25

The tongue of the righteous is pure silver;
the heart of the wicked is of little value.

Proverbs 10:20

Anxiety in a person's heart weighs it down,
but a good word cheers it up.

Proverbs 12:25

Hope delayed makes the heart sick,
but desire fulfilled is a tree of life.

Proverbs 13:12

The heart knows its own bitterness,
and no outsider shares in its joy.

Proverbs 14:10

A tranquil heart is life to the body,
but jealousy is rottenness to the bones.

Proverbs 14:30

Wisdom resides in the heart of the discerning;
she is known even among fools.

Proverbs 14:33

The lips of the wise broadcast knowledge,
but not so the heart of fools.

Proverbs 15:7

Sheol and Abaddon lie open before the LORD—
how much more, human hearts.

Proverbs 15:11

A joyful heart makes a face cheerful,
but a sad heart produces a broken spirit.

Proverbs 15:13

Bright eyes cheer the heart;
good news strengthens the bones.

Proverbs 15:30

The reflections of the heart belong to mankind,
but the answer of the tongue is from the LORD.

Proverbs 16:1

Everyone with a proud heart is detestable to the LORD;
be assured, he will not go unpunished.

Proverbs 16:5

A person's heart plans his way,
but the LORD determines his steps.

Proverbs 16:9

Anyone with a wise heart is called discerning,
and pleasant speech increases learning.

Proverbs 16:21

The heart of a wise person instructs his mouth;
it adds learning to his speech.

Proverbs 16:23

A crucible for silver, and a smelter for gold,
and the LORD is the tester of hearts.

Proverbs 17:3

A joyful heart is good medicine,
but a broken spirit dries up the bones.

Proverbs 17:22

Before his downfall a person's heart is proud,
but humility comes before honor.

Proverbs 18:12

A person's own foolishness leads him astray,
yet his heart rages against the LORD.

Proverbs 19:3

Many plans are in a person's heart,
but the LORD's decree will prevail.

Proverbs 19:21

Counsel in a person's heart is deep water;
but a person of understanding draws it out.

Proverbs 20:5

Who can say, "I have kept my heart pure;
I am cleansed from my sin"?

Proverbs 20:9

A king's heart is like channeled water in the LORD's
hand:
He directs it wherever he chooses.

Proverbs 21:1

All a person's ways seem right to him,
but the LORD weighs hearts.

Proverbs 21:2

Foolishness is bound to the heart of a youth;
a rod of discipline will separate it from him.

Proverbs 22:15

My son, if your heart is wise,
my heart will indeed rejoice.
My innermost being will celebrate
when your lips say what is right.

Proverbs 23:15-16

My son, give me your heart,
and let your eyes observe my ways.

Proverbs 23:26

Don't gloat when your enemy falls,
and don't let your heart rejoice when he stumbles,
or the LORD will see, be displeased,
and turn his wrath away from him.

Proverbs 24:17-18

I saw, and took it to heart;
I looked, and received instruction.

Proverbs 24:32

If you do nothing in a difficult time,
your strength is limited.
Rescue those being taken off to death,
and save those stumbling toward slaughter.
If you say, "But we didn't know about this,"
won't he who weighs hearts consider it?
Won't he who protects your life know?
Won't he repay a person according to his work?

Proverbs 24:10-12

As the heavens are high and the earth is deep,
so the hearts of kings cannot be investigated.

Proverbs 25:3

Smooth lips with an evil heart
are like glaze on an earthen vessel.

Proverbs 26:23

As water reflects the face,
so the heart reflects the person.

Proverbs 27:19

Happy is the one who is always reverent,
but one who hardens his heart falls into trouble.

Proverbs 28:14

Who can find a wife of noble character?
She is far more precious than jewels.
The heart of her husband trusts in her,
and he will not lack anything good.

Proverbs 31:10-11

Honesty

Don't let your mouth speak dishonestly,
and don't let your lips talk deviously.

Proverbs 4:24

Whoever speaks the truth declares what is right,
but a false witness speaks deceit.

Proverbs 12:17

An honest witness does not deceive,
but a dishonest witness utters lies.

Proverbs 14:5

A truthful witness rescues lives,
but one who utters lies is deceitful.

Proverbs 14:25

The one who profits dishonestly troubles his household,
but the one who hates bribes will live.

Proverbs 15:27

Righteous lips are a king's delight,
and he loves one who speaks honestly.

Proverbs 16:13

It is certainly not good to fine an innocent person
or to beat a noble for his honesty.

Proverbs 17:26

Don't move an ancient boundary marker
that your fathers set up.

Proverbs 22:28

Don't move an ancient boundary marker,
and don't encroach on the fields of the fatherless,
for their Redeemer is strong,
and he will champion their cause against you.

Proverbs 23:10-11

He who gives an honest answer
gives a kiss on the lips.

Proverbs 24:26

The one who conceals his sins
will not prosper,
but whoever confesses and renounces them
will find mercy.

Proverbs 28:13

Bloodthirsty men hate an honest person,
but the upright care about him.

Proverbs 29:10

Honor

Long life is in her [Wisdom's] right hand;
in her left, riches and honor.

Proverbs 3:16

The wise will inherit honor,
but he holds up fools to dishonor.

Proverbs 3:35

Cherish her [Understanding], and she will exalt you;
if you embrace her, she will honor you.

Proverbs 4:8

With me [Wisdom] are riches and honor,
lasting wealth and righteousness.

Proverbs 8:18

The way of the LORD is a stronghold for the honorable,
but destruction awaits the malicious.

Proverbs 10:29

A gracious woman gains honor,
but violent people gain only riches.

Proverbs 11:16

Poverty and disgrace come to those
who ignore discipline,
but the one who accepts correction will be honored.

Proverbs 13:18

The one who oppresses the poor person insults his
Maker,
but one who is kind to the needy honors him.

Proverbs 14:31

The fear of the LORD is what wisdom teaches,
and humility comes before honor.

Proverbs 15:33

Before his downfall a person's heart is proud,
but humility comes before honor.

Proverbs 18:12

Honor belongs to the person who ends a dispute,
but any fool can get himself into a quarrel.

Proverbs 20:3

The one who pursues righteousness and faithful love
will find life, righteousness, and honor.

Proverbs 21:21

Humility, the fear of the LORD,
results in wealth, honor, and life.

Proverbs 22:4

Like snow in summer and rain at harvest,
honor is inappropriate for a fool.

Proverbs 26:1

Whoever tends a fig tree will eat its fruit,
and whoever looks after his master will be honored.

Proverbs 27:18

A person's pride will humble him,
but a humble spirit will gain honor.

Proverbs 29:23

Hope

The hope of the righteous is joy,
but the expectation of the wicked will perish.

Proverbs 10:28

When the wicked person dies,
his expectation comes to nothing,
and hope placed in wealth vanishes.

Proverbs 11:7

The desire of the righteous turns out well,
but the hope of the wicked leads to wrath.

Proverbs 11:23

Hope delayed makes the heart sick,
but desire fulfilled is a tree of life.

Proverbs 13:12

Discipline your son while there is hope;
don't set your heart on being the cause of his death.

Proverbs 19:18

Don't let your heart envy sinners;
instead, always fear the LORD.
For then you will have a future,
and your hope will not be dashed.

Proverbs 23:17-18

If you find it [Wisdom], you will have a future,
and your hope will never fade.

Proverbs 24:14b

Do you see a person who is wise in his own eyes?
There is more hope for a fool than for him.

Proverbs 26:12

Humility

Don't be wise in your own eyes;
fear the LORD and turn away from evil.
This will be healing for your body
and strengthening for your bones.

Proverbs 3:7-8

He mocks those who mock,
but gives grace to the humble.

Proverbs 3:34

When arrogance comes, disgrace follows,
but with humility comes wisdom.

Proverbs 11:2

Arrogance leads to nothing but strife,
but wisdom is gained by those who take advice.

Proverbs 13:10

Better to be disregarded, yet have a servant,
than to act important but have no food.

Proverbs 12:9

The fear of the LORD is what wisdom teaches,
and humility comes before honor.

Proverbs 15:33

Better to be lowly of spirit with the humble
than to divide plunder with the proud.

Proverbs 16:19

Before his downfall a person's heart is proud,
but humility comes before honor.

Proverbs 18:12

Humility, the fear of the LORD,
results in wealth, honor, and life.

Proverbs 22:4

Don't gloat when your enemy falls,
and don't let your heart rejoice when he stumbles,
or the LORD will see, be displeased,
and turn his wrath away from him.

Proverbs 24:17-18

Don't boast about yourself before the king,
and don't stand in the place of the great;
for it is better for him to say to you, "Come up here!"
than to demote you in plain view of a noble.

Proverbs 25:6-7

Let another praise you, and not your own mouth—
a stranger, and not your own lips.

Proverbs 27:2

A crucible refines silver, a smelter refines gold,
and a person refines his praise.

Proverbs 27:21

A person's pride will humble him,
but a humble spirit will gain honor.

Proverbs 29:23

Impulsiveness

A fool's displeasure is known at once,
but whoever ignores an insult is sensible.

Proverbs 12:16

There is one who speaks rashly,
like a piercing sword;
but the tongue of the wise brings healing.

Proverbs 12:18

A quick-tempered person acts foolishly,
and one who schemes is hated.

Proverbs 14:17

A patient person shows great understanding,
but a quick-tempered one promotes foolishness.

Proverbs 14:29

The tongue of the wise makes knowledge attractive,
but the mouth of fools blurts out foolishness.

Proverbs 15:2

A hot-tempered person stirs up conflict,
but one slow to anger calms strife.

Proverbs 15:18

The mind of the righteous person thinks before answering,
but the mouth of the wicked blurts out evil things.

Proverbs 15:28

Even a fool is considered wise when he keeps silent—
discerning, when he seals his lips.

Proverbs 17:28

The one who gives an answer before he listens—
this is foolishness and disgrace for him.

Proverbs 18:13

Even zeal is not good without knowledge,
and the one who acts hastily sins.

Proverbs 19:2

Don't say, "I will avenge this evil!"
Wait on the LORD, and he will rescue you.

Proverbs 20:22

It is a trap for anyone to dedicate something rashly
and later to reconsider his vows.

Proverbs 20:25

The plans of the diligent certainly lead to profit,
but anyone who is reckless certainly becomes poor.

Proverbs 21:5

Better to live in a wilderness
than with a nagging and hot-tempered wife.

Proverbs 21:19

A fool gives full vent to his anger,
but a wise person holds it in check.

Proverbs 29:11

Do you see someone who speaks too soon?
There is more hope for a fool than for him.

Proverbs 29:20

An angry person stirs up conflict,
and a hot-tempered one increases rebellion.

Proverbs 29:22

Inexperience

How long will you mockers enjoy mocking
and you fools hate knowledge?

Proverbs 1:22

For the apostasy of the inexperienced will kill them,
and the complacency of fools will destroy them.

Proverbs 1:32

At the window of my house
I looked through my lattice.
I saw among the inexperienced,
I noticed among the youths,
a young man lacking sense.
Crossing the street near her corner,
he strolled down the road to her house
at twilight, in the evening,
in the dark of the night.
A woman came to meet him

dressed like a prostitute,
having a hidden agenda.

Proverbs 7:6-10

Learn to be shrewd, you who are inexperienced;
develop common sense, you who are foolish.

Proverbs 8:5

[Wisdom] has sent out her female servants;
she calls out from the highest points of the city:
"Whoever is inexperienced, enter here!"
To the one who lacks sense, she says,
"Come, eat my bread,
and drink the wine I have mixed.
Leave inexperience behind, and you will live;
pursue the way of understanding."

Proverbs 9:3-6

The inexperienced one believes anything,
but the sensible one watches his steps.

Proverbs 14:15

The inexperienced inherit foolishness,
but the sensible are crowned with knowledge.

Proverbs 14:18

Strike a mocker, and the inexperienced learn a lesson;
rebuke the discerning, and he gains knowledge.

Proverbs 19:25

When a mocker is punished,
the inexperienced become wiser;
when one teaches a wise man,
he acquires knowledge.

Proverbs 21:11

A sensible person sees danger and takes cover,
but the inexperienced keep going and are punished.

Proverbs 22:3, 27:12

Integrity

For the upright will inhabit the land,
and those of integrity will remain in it;
but the wicked will be cut off from the land,
and the treacherous ripped out of it.

Proverbs 2:21-22

The one who lives with integrity lives securely,
but whoever perverts his ways will be found out.

Proverbs 10:9

The integrity of the upright guides them,
but the perversity of the treacherous destroys them.

Proverbs 11:3

A gossip goes around revealing a secret,
but a trustworthy person keeps a confidence.

Proverbs 11:13

Righteousness guards people of integrity,
but wickedness undermines the sinner.

Proverbs 13:6

A wicked envoy falls into trouble,
but a trustworthy courier brings healing.

Proverbs 13:17

Whoever lives with integrity fears the LORD,
but the one who is devious in his ways despises him.

Proverbs 14:2

The disloyal one will get what his conduct deserves,
and a good one, what his deeds deserve.

Proverbs 14:14

Better a poor person who lives with integrity
than someone who has deceitful lips and is a fool.

Proverbs 19:1

Many a person proclaims his own loyalty,
but who can find a trustworthy person?

Proverbs 20:6

A righteous person acts with integrity;
his children who come after him will be happy.

Proverbs 20:7

A good name is to be chosen over great wealth;
favor is better than silver and gold.

Proverbs 22:1

To those who send him, a trustworthy envoy
is like the coolness of snow on a harvest day;
he refreshes the life of his masters.

Proverbs 25:13

Trusting an unreliable person in a difficult time
is like a rotten tooth or a faltering foot.

Proverbs 25:19

Better the poor person who lives with integrity
than the rich one who distorts right and wrong.

Proverbs 28:6

The one who lives with integrity will be helped,
but one who distorts right and wrong
will suddenly fall.

Proverbs 28:18

Don't slander a servant to his master
or he will curse you, and you will become guilty.

Proverbs 30:10

Justice

He is a shield for those who live with integrity
so that he may guard the paths of justice
and protect the way of his faithful followers.

Proverbs 2:7b-8

When it is in your power,
don't withhold good from the one to whom it belongs.
Don't say to your neighbor, "Go away! Come back later.
I'll give it tomorrow"—when it is there with you.
Don't plan any harm against your neighbor,
for he trusts you and lives near you.
Don't accuse anyone without cause,
when he has done you no harm.

Proverbs 3:27-30

I [Wisdom] walk in the ways of righteousness,
along the paths of justice,
giving wealth as an inheritance to those who love me,
and filling their treasuries.

Proverbs 8:20-21

Dishonest scales are detestable to the LORD,
but an accurate weight is his delight.

Proverbs 11:1

The uncultivated field of the poor yields abundant food,
but without justice, it is swept away.

Proverbs 13:23

The LORD tears apart the house of the proud,
but he protects the widow's territory.

Proverbs 15:25

Better a little with righteousness
than great income with injustice.

Proverbs 16:8

God's verdict is on the lips of a king;
his mouth should not give an unfair judgment.

Proverbs 16:10

Honest balances and scales are the LORD's;
all the weights in the bag are his concern.

Proverbs 16:11

Acquitting the guilty and condemning the just—
both are detestable to the LORD.

Proverbs 17:15

A wicked person secretly takes a bribe
to subvert the course of justice.

Proverbs 17:23

It is certainly not good to fine an innocent person
or to beat a noble for his honesty.

Proverbs 17:26

It is not good to show partiality to the guilty,
denying an innocent person justice.

Proverbs 18:5

A worthless witness mocks justice,
and a wicked mouth swallows iniquity.

Proverbs 19:28

Differing weights and varying measures—
both are detestable to the LORD.

Proverbs 20:10

Differing weights are detestable to the LORD,
and dishonest scales are unfair.

Proverbs 20:23

Doing what is righteous and just
is more acceptable to the LORD than sacrifice.

Proverbs 21:3

The violence of the wicked sweeps them away
because they refuse to act justly.

Proverbs 21:7

Justice executed is a joy to the righteous
but a terror to those who practice iniquity.

Proverbs 21:15

The one who sows injustice will reap disaster,
and the rod of his fury will be destroyed.

Proverbs 22:8

Oppressing the poor to enrich oneself,
and giving to the rich—both lead only to poverty.

Proverbs 22:16

These sayings also belong to the wise:
It is not good to show partiality in judgment.
Whoever says to the guilty, "You are innocent"—
peoples will curse him, and nations will denounce him;
but it will go well with those who convict the guilty,
and a generous blessing will come to them.

Proverbs 24:23-25

Don't testify against your neighbor without cause.
Don't deceive with your lips.

Don't say, "I'll do to him what he did to me;
I'll repay the man for what he has done."

Proverbs 24:28-29

Like a flitting sparrow or a fluttering swallow,
an undeserved curse goes nowhere.

Proverbs 26:2

The evil do not understand justice,
but those who seek the LORD understand everything.

Proverbs 28:5

It is not good to show partiality—
yet even a courageous person may sin for a piece of
bread.

Proverbs 28:21

By justice a king brings stability to a land,
but a person who demands "contributions"
demolishes it.

Proverbs 29:4

A king who judges the poor with fairness—
his throne will be established forever.

Proverbs 29:14

Many desire a ruler's favor,
but a person receives justice from the LORD.

Proverbs 29:26

Speak up for those who have no voice,
for the justice of all who are dispossessed.
Speak up, judge righteously,
and defend the cause of the oppressed and needy.

Proverbs 31:8-9

Kindness

A kind man benefits himself,
but a cruel person brings ruin on himself.

Proverbs 11:17

One person gives freely,
yet gains more;
another withholds what is right,
only to become poor.

Proverbs 11:24

A generous person will be enriched,
and the one who gives a drink of water
will receive water.

Proverbs 11:25

The righteous cares about his animal's health,
but even the merciful acts of the wicked are cruel.

Proverbs 12:10

The one who despises his neighbor sins,
but whoever shows kindness to the poor will be happy.

Proverbs 14:21

The one who oppresses the poor person insults his Maker,
but one who is kind to the needy honors him.

Proverbs 14:31

Kindness to the poor is a loan to the LORD,
and he will give a reward to the lender.

Proverbs 19:17

A slacker's craving will kill him
because his hands refuse to work.
He is filled with craving all day long,
but the righteous give and don't hold back.

Proverbs 21:25-26

A generous person will be blessed,
for he shares his food with the poor.

Proverbs 22:9

If your enemy is hungry, give him food to eat,
and if he is thirsty, give him water to drink;
for you will heap burning coals on his head,
and the LORD will reward you.

Proverbs 25:21-22

Whoever increases his wealth through excessive interest
collects it for one who is kind to the poor.

Proverbs 28:8

The one who gives to the poor
will not be in need,
but one who turns his eyes away
will receive many curses.

Proverbs 28:27

[The noble wife's] hands reach out to the poor,
and she extends her hands to the needy.

Proverbs 31:20

Knowledge

The fear of the LORD
is the beginning of knowledge;
fools despise wisdom and discipline.

Proverbs 1:7

How long, inexperienced ones, will you love ignorance?
How long will you mockers enjoy mocking
and you fools hate knowledge?

Proverbs 1:22

My son, if you accept my words
and store up my commands within you,
listening closely to wisdom
and directing your heart to understanding;
furthermore, if you call out to insight
and lift your voice to understanding,
if you seek it like silver
and search for it like hidden treasure,
then you will understand the fear of the LORD
and discover the knowledge of God.

Proverbs 2:1-5

And whatever else you get, get understanding.
Cherish her, and she will exalt you;
if you embrace her, she will honor you.

She will place a garland of favor on your head;
she will give you a crown of beauty.

Proverbs 4:7b-9

My son, pay attention to my wisdom;
listen closely to my understanding
so that you may maintain discretion
and your lips safeguard knowledge.

Proverbs 5:1-2

Accept my instruction instead of silver,
and knowledge rather than pure gold.

Proverbs 8:10

I, wisdom, share a home with shrewdness
and have knowledge and discretion.

Proverbs 8:12

The wise store up knowledge,
but the mouth of the fool hastens destruction.

Proverbs 10:14

With his mouth the ungodly destroys his neighbor,
but through knowledge the righteous are rescued.

Proverbs 11:9

A man is praised for his insight,
but a twisted mind is despised.

Proverbs 12:8

Good sense wins favor,
but the way of the treacherous never changes.

Proverbs 13:15

Every sensible person acts knowledgeably,
but a fool displays his stupidity.

Proverbs 13:16

A mocker seeks wisdom and doesn't find it,
but knowledge comes easily to the perceptive.

Proverbs 14:6

Stay away from a foolish person;
you will gain no knowledge from his speech.

Proverbs 14:7

The inexperienced inherit foolishness,
but the sensible are crowned with knowledge.

Proverbs 14:18

The tongue of the wise makes knowledge attractive,
but the mouth of fools blurts out foolishness.

Proverbs 15:2

The lips of the wise broadcast knowledge,
but not so the heart of fools.

Proverbs 15:7

A discerning mind seeks knowledge,
but the mouth of fools feeds on foolishness.

Proverbs 15:14

Foolishness brings joy to one without sense,
but a person with understanding walks a straight path.

Proverbs 15:21

Get wisdom—
how much better it is than gold!
And get understanding—
it is preferable to silver.

Proverbs 16:16

Insight is a fountain of life for its possessor,
but the discipline of fools is folly.

Proverbs 16:22

The one who has knowledge restrains his words,
and one who keeps a cool head
is a person of understanding.

Proverbs 17:27

A fool does not delight in understanding,
but only wants to show off his opinions.

Proverbs 18:2

The mind of the discerning acquires knowledge,
and the ear of the wise seeks it.

Proverbs 18:15

Even zeal is not good without knowledge,
and the one who acts hastily sins.

Proverbs 19:2

The one who acquires good sense loves himself;
one who safeguards understanding finds success.

Proverbs 19:8

A person's insight gives him patience,
and his virtue is to overlook an offense.

Proverbs 19:11

Strike a mocker, and the inexperienced learn a lesson;
rebuke the discerning, and he gains knowledge.

Proverbs 19:25

If you stop listening to correction, my son,
you will stray from the words of knowledge.

Proverbs 19:27

There is gold and a multitude of jewels,
but knowledgeable lips are a rare treasure.

Proverbs 20:15

When a mocker is punished,
the inexperienced become wiser;
when one teaches a wise man,
he acquires knowledge.

Proverbs 21:11

The LORD's eyes keep watch over knowledge,
but he overthrows the words of the treacherous.

Proverbs 22:12

Apply yourself to discipline
and listen to words of knowledge.

Proverbs 23:12

Buy—and do not sell—truth,
wisdom, instruction, and understanding.

Proverbs 23:23

A house is built by wisdom,
and it is established by understanding;
by knowledge the rooms are filled
with every precious and beautiful treasure.

Proverbs 24:3-4

A wise warrior is better than a strong one,
and a man of knowledge than one of strength;
for you should wage war with sound guidance—
victory comes with many counselors.

Proverbs 24:5-6

It is the glory of God to conceal a matter
and the glory of kings to investigate a matter.

Proverbs 25:2

When a land is in rebellion, it has many rulers,
but with a discerning and knowledgeable person, it
endures.

Proverbs 28:2

The evil do not understand justice,
but those who seek the LORD understand everything.

Proverbs 28:5

Laziness

Go to the ant, you slacker!
Observe its ways and become wise.
Without leader, administrator, or ruler,
it prepares its provisions in summer;
it gathers its food during harvest.
How long will you stay in bed, you slacker?
When will you get up from your sleep?
A little sleep, a little slumber,
a little folding of the arms to rest,
and your poverty will come like a robber,
your need, like a bandit.

Proverbs 6:6-11

Idle hands make one poor,
but diligent hands bring riches.

Proverbs 10:4

The son who gathers during summer is prudent;
the son who sleeps during harvest is disgraceful.

Proverbs 10:5

Like vinegar to the teeth and smoke to the eyes,
so the slacker is to the one who sends him on an errand.

Proverbs 10:26

The one who works his land will have plenty of food,
but whoever chases fantasies lacks sense.

Proverbs 12:11

The diligent hand will rule,
but laziness will lead to forced labor.

Proverbs 12:24

A lazy hunter doesn't roast his game,
but to a diligent person, his wealth is precious.

Proverbs 12:27

The slacker craves, yet has nothing,
but the diligent is fully satisfied.

Proverbs 13:4

A slacker's way is like a thorny hedge,
but the path of the upright is a highway.

Proverbs 15:19

The one who is lazy in his work
is brother to a vandal.

Proverbs 18:9

Laziness induces deep sleep,
and a lazy person will go hungry.

Proverbs 19:15

The slacker buries his hand in the bowl;
he doesn't even bring it back to his mouth!

Proverbs 19:24

The slacker does not plow during planting season;
at harvest time he looks, and there is nothing.

Proverbs 20:4

Don't love sleep, or you will become poor;
open your eyes, and you'll have enough to eat.

Proverbs 20:13

A slacker's craving will kill him
because his hands refuse to work.
He is filled with craving all day long,
but the righteous give and don't hold back.

Proverbs 21:25-26

The slacker says, "There's a lion outside!
I'll be killed in the public square!"

Proverbs 22:13

I went by the field of a slacker
and by the vineyard of one lacking sense.
Thistles had come up everywhere,
weeds covered the ground,
and the stone wall was ruined.
I saw, and took it to heart;
I looked, and received instruction:
a little sleep, a little slumber,
a little folding of the arms to rest,
and your poverty will come like a robber,
and your need, like a bandit.

Proverbs 24:30-34

The slacker says, "There's a lion in the road—
a lion in the public square!"
A door turns on its hinges,
and a slacker, on his bed.
The slacker buries his hand in the bowl;
he is too weary to bring it to his mouth!
In his own eyes, a slacker is wiser
than seven who can answer sensibly.

Proverbs 26:13-16

The one who works his land
will have plenty of food,
but whoever chases fantasies
will have his fill of poverty.

Proverbs 28:19

Life

My son, don't forget my teaching,
but let your heart keep my commands;
for they will bring you
many days, a full life, and well-being.

Proverbs 3:1-2

Long life is in her [Wisdom's] right hand;
in her left, riches and honor.

Proverbs 3:16

She [Wisdom] is a tree of life to those who embrace her,
and those who hold on to her are happy.

Proverbs 3:18

Maintain sound wisdom and discretion.
My son, don't lose sight of them.
They will be life for you
and adornment for your neck.

Proverbs 3:21-22

When I was a son with my father,
tender and precious to my mother,
he taught me and said:
"Your heart must hold on to my words.
Keep my commands and live."

Proverbs 4:3-4

Listen, my son. Accept my words,
and you will live many years.

Proverbs 4:10

Hold on to instruction; don't let go.
Guard it, for it is your life.

Proverbs 4:13

My son, pay attention to my words;
listen closely to my sayings.
Don't lose sight of them;
keep them within your heart.
For they are life to those who find them,
and health to one's whole body.

Proverbs 4:20-22

She [the forbidden woman] doesn't consider the path
of life;
she doesn't know that her ways are unstable.

Proverbs 5:6

For the one who finds me [Wisdom] finds life
and obtains favor from the LORD,
but the one who misses me harms himself;
all who hate me love death.

Proverbs 8:35-36

For by me your days will be many,
and years will be added to your life.

Proverbs 9:11

The mouth of the righteous is a fountain of life,
but the mouth of the wicked conceals violence.

Proverbs 10:11

The reward of the righteous is life;
the wages of the wicked is punishment.

Proverbs 10:16

The fear of the LORD prolongs life,
but the years of the wicked are cut short.

Proverbs 10:27

Genuine righteousness leads to life,
but pursuing evil leads to death.

Proverbs 11:19

The fruit of the righteous is a tree of life,
and a wise person captivates people.

Proverbs 11:30

There is life in the path of righteousness,
and in its path there is no death.

Proverbs 12:28

The one who guards his mouth protects his life;
the one who opens his lips invites his own ruin.

Proverbs 13:3

Hope delayed makes the heart sick,
but desire fulfilled is a tree of life.

Proverbs 13:12

A wise person's instruction is a fountain of life,
turning people away from the snares of death.

Proverbs 13:14

The fear of the LORD is a fountain of life,
turning people away from the snares of death.

Proverbs 14:27

A tranquil heart is life to the body,
but jealousy is rottenness to the bones.

Proverbs 14:30

The tongue that heals is a tree of life,
but a devious tongue breaks the spirit.

Proverbs 15:4

One who listens to life-giving rebukes
will be at home among the wise.

Proverbs 15:31

When a king's face lights up, there is life;
his favor is like a cloud with spring rain.

Proverbs 16:15

Insight is a fountain of life for its possessor,
but the discipline of fools is folly.

Proverbs 16:22

Death and life are in the power of the tongue,
and those who love it will eat its fruit.

Proverbs 18:21

The fear of the LORD leads to life;
one will sleep at night without danger.

Proverbs 19:23

Humility, the fear of the LORD,
results in wealth, honor, and life.

Proverbs 22:4

A leader who lacks understanding
is very oppressive,
but one who hates dishonest profit
prolongs his life.

Proverbs 28:16

Grandchildren are the crown of the elderly,
and the pride of children is their fathers.

Proverbs 17:6

Love

Do not despise the LORD's instruction, my son,
and do not loathe his discipline;
for the LORD disciplines the one he loves,
just as a father disciplines the son in whom he delights.

Proverbs 3:11-12

Hatred stirs up conflicts,
but love covers all offenses.

Proverbs 10:12

A wife of noble character is her husband's crown,
but a wife who causes shame
is like rottenness in his bones.

Proverbs 12:4

The one who will not use the rod hates his son,
but the one who loves him disciplines him diligently.

Proverbs 13:24

Better a meal of vegetables where there is love
than a fattened ox with hatred.

Proverbs 15:17

Whoever conceals an offense promotes love,
but whoever gossips about it separates friends.

Proverbs 17:9

A friend loves at all times,
and a brother is born for a difficult time.

Proverbs 17:17

The one who pursues righteousness and faithful love
will find life, righteousness, and honor.

Proverbs 21:21

Better an open reprimand
than concealed love.

Proverbs 27:5

Lying

The LORD hates six things;
in fact, seven are detestable to him:
arrogant eyes, a lying tongue,
hands that shed innocent blood,
a heart that plots wicked schemes,
feet eager to run to evil,
a lying witness who gives false testimony,
and one who stirs up trouble among brothers.

Proverbs 6:16-19

The one who conceals hatred has lying lips,
and whoever spreads slander is a fool.

Proverbs 10:18

Whoever speaks the truth declares what is right,
but a false witness speaks deceit.

Proverbs 12:17

Truthful lips endure forever,
but a lying tongue, only a moment.

Proverbs 12:19

Lying lips are detestable to the LORD,
but faithful people are his delight.

Proverbs 12:22

The righteous hate lying,
but the wicked bring disgust and shame.

Proverbs 13:5

An honest witness does not deceive,
but a dishonest witness utters lies.

Proverbs 14:5

A truthful witness rescues lives,
but one who utters lies is deceitful.

Proverbs 14:25

A wicked person listens to malicious talk;
a liar pays attention to a destructive tongue.

Proverbs 17:4

Better a poor person who lives with integrity
than someone who has deceitful lips and is a fool.

Proverbs 19:1

A false witness will not go unpunished,
and one who utters lies will not escape.

Proverbs 19:5

A false witness will not go unpunished,
and one who utters lies perishes.

Proverbs 19:9

What is desirable in a person is his fidelity;
better to be a poor person than a liar.

Proverbs 19:22

Making a fortune through a lying tongue
is a vanishing mist, a pursuit of death.

Proverbs 21:6

A lying witness will perish,
but the one who listens will speak successfully.

Proverbs 21:28

The one who boasts about a gift that does not exist
is like clouds and wind without rain.

Proverbs 25:14

A person giving false testimony against his neighbor
is like a club, a sword, or a sharp arrow.
Trusting an unreliable person in a difficult time
is like a rotten tooth or a faltering foot.

Proverbs 25:18-19

A lying tongue hates those it crushes,
and a flattering mouth causes ruin.

Proverbs 26:28

If a ruler listens to lies,
all his officials will be wicked.

Proverbs 29:12

Marriage

Drink water from your own cistern,
water flowing from your own well.
Should your springs flow in the streets,
streams in the public squares?
They should be for you alone
and not for you to share with strangers.
Let your fountain be blessed,
and take pleasure in the wife of your youth.
A loving deer, a graceful doe—
let her breasts always satisfy you;
be lost in her love forever.
Why, my son, would you lose yourself
with a forbidden woman
or embrace a wayward woman?

Proverbs 5:15-20

A wife of noble character is her husband's crown,
but a wife who causes shame
is like rottenness in his bones.

Proverbs 12:4

A man who finds a wife finds a good thing
and obtains favor from the LORD.

Proverbs 18:22

A foolish son is his father's ruin,
and a wife's nagging is an endless dripping.

Proverbs 19:13

A house and wealth are inherited from fathers,
but a prudent wife is from the LORD.

Proverbs 19:14

Better to live on the corner of a roof
than to share a house with a nagging wife.

Proverbs 21:9, 25:24

Better to live in a wilderness
than with a nagging and hot-tempered wife.

Proverbs 21:19

An endless dripping on a rainy day
and a nagging wife are alike;
the one who controls her controls the wind
and grasps oil with his right hand.

Proverbs 27:15-16

Who can find a wife of noble character?
She is far more precious than jewels.
The heart of her husband trusts in her,
and he will not lack anything good.
She rewards him with good, not evil,
all the days of her life.
She selects wool and flax
and works with willing hands.
She is like the merchant ships,
bringing her food from far away.
She rises while it is still night
and provides food for her household
and portions for her female servants.
She evaluates a field and buys it;
she plants a vineyard with her earnings.
She draws on her strength

and reveals that her arms are strong.
She sees that her profits are good,
and her lamp never goes out at night.
She extends her hands to the spinning staff,
and her hands hold the spindle.
Her hands reach out to the poor,
and she extends her hands to the needy.
She is not afraid for her household when it snows,
for all in her household are doubly clothed.
She makes her own bed coverings;
her clothing is fine linen and purple.
Her husband is known at the city gates,
where he sits among the elders of the land.
She makes and sells linen garments;
she delivers belts to the merchants.
Strength and honor are her clothing,
and she can laugh at the time to come.
Her mouth speaks wisdom,
and loving instruction is on her tongue.
She watches over the activities of her household
and is never idle.
Her children rise up and call her blessed;
her husband also praises her:
"Many women have done noble deeds,
but you surpass them all!"
Charm is deceptive and beauty is fleeting,
but a woman who fears the LORD will be praised.
Give her the reward of her labor,
and let her works praise her at the city gates.

Proverbs 31:10-31

Money

The wealth of the rich is his fortified city;
the poverty of the poor is their destruction.

Proverbs 10:15

One person gives freely,
yet gains more;
another withholds what is right,
only to become poor.

Proverbs 11:24

Poverty and disgrace come to those
who ignore discipline,
but the one who accepts correction will be honored.

Proverbs 13:18

The uncultivated field of the poor yields abundant food,
but without justice, it is swept away.

Proverbs 13:23

A poor person is hated even by his neighbor,
but there are many who love the rich.

Proverbs 14:20

There is profit in all hard work,
but endless talk leads only to poverty.

Proverbs 14:23

The poor person pleads,
but the rich one answers roughly.

Proverbs 18:23

Wealth attracts many friends,
but a poor person is separated from his friend.

Proverbs 19:4

All the brothers of a poor person hate him;
how much more do his friends
keep their distance from him!
He may pursue them with words,
but they are not there.

Proverbs 19:7

Don't love sleep, or you will become poor;
open your eyes, and you'll have enough to eat.

Proverbs 20:13

The one who shuts his ears to the cry of the poor
will himself also call out and not be answered.

Proverbs 21:13

Rich and poor have this in common:
the LORD makes them all.

Proverbs 22:2

The rich rule over the poor,
and the borrower is a slave to the lender.

Proverbs 22:7

Oppressing the poor to enrich oneself,
and giving to the rich—both lead only to poverty.

Proverbs 22:16

Don't rob a poor person because he is poor,
and don't crush the oppressed at the city gate,
for the LORD will champion their cause
and will plunder those who plunder them.

Proverbs 22:22-23

I went by the field of a slacker
and by the vineyard of one lacking sense.
Thistles had come up everywhere,
weeds covered the ground,
and the stone wall was ruined.
I saw, and took it to heart;
I looked, and received instruction:
a little sleep, a little slumber,
a little folding of the arms to rest,
and your poverty will come like a robber,
and your need, like a bandit.

Proverbs 24:30-34

The one who works his land
will have plenty of food,
but whoever chases fantasies
will have his fill of poverty.

Proverbs 28:19

The poor and the oppressor have this in common:
the LORD gives light to the eyes of both.

Proverbs 29:13

Give me neither poverty nor wealth;
feed me with the food I need.
Otherwise, I might have too much
and deny you, saying, "Who is the LORD?"
or I might have nothing and steal,
profaning the name of my God.

Proverbs 30:8b-9

Motives

For a man's ways are before the LORD's eyes,
and he considers all his paths.

Proverbs 5:21

The eyes of the LORD are everywhere,
observing the wicked and the good.

Proverbs 15:3

Sheol and Abaddon lie open before the LORD—
how much more, human hearts.

Proverbs 15:11

All a person's ways seem right to him,
but the LORD weighs motives.

Proverbs 16:2

A crucible for silver, and a smelter for gold,
and the LORD is the tester of hearts.

Proverbs 17:3

The LORD's lamp sheds light on a person's life,
searching the innermost parts.

Proverbs 20:27

Lashes and wounds purge away evil,
and beatings cleanse the innermost parts.

Proverbs 20:30

The sacrifice of a wicked person is detestable—
how much more so
when he brings it with ulterior motives!

Proverbs 21:27

If you do nothing in a difficult time,
your strength is limited.
Rescue those being taken off to death,
and save those stumbling toward slaughter.
If you say, "But we didn't know about this,"
won't he who weighs hearts consider it?
Won't he who protects your life know?
Won't he repay a person according to his work?

Proverbs 24:10-12

Neighbors

Don't say to your neighbor, "Go away! Come back later.
I'll give it tomorrow"—when it is there with you.
Don't plan any harm against your neighbor,
for he trusts you and lives near you.

Proverbs 3:28-29

With his mouth the ungodly destroys his neighbor,
but through knowledge the righteous are rescued.

Proverbs 11:9

Whoever shows contempt for his neighbor lacks sense,
but a person with understanding keeps silent.

Proverbs 11:12

A righteous person is careful in dealing with his neighbor,
but the ways of the wicked lead them astray.

Proverbs 12:26

A poor person is hated even by his neighbor,
but there are many who love the rich.

Proverbs 14:20

The one who despises his neighbor sins,
but whoever shows kindness to the poor will be happy.

Proverbs 14:21

A violent person lures his neighbor,
leading him on a path that is not good.

Proverbs 16:29

A wicked person desires evil;
he has no consideration for his neighbor.

Proverbs 21:10

Don't testify against your neighbor without cause.
Don't deceive with your lips.
Don't say, "I'll do to him what he did to me;
I'll repay the man for what he has done."

Proverbs 24:28-29

Seldom set foot in your neighbor's house;
otherwise, he'll get sick of you and hate you.

Proverbs 25:17

A person giving false testimony against his neighbor
is like a club, a sword, or a sharp arrow.

Proverbs 25:18

Like a madman who throws flaming darts and deadly
arrows,
so is the person who deceives his neighbor
and says, "I was only joking!"

Proverbs 26:18-19

Don't abandon your friend or your father's friend,
and don't go to your brother's house
in your time of calamity;
better a neighbor nearby than a brother far away.

Proverbs 27:10

If one blesses his neighbor
with a loud voice early in the morning,
it will be counted as a curse to him.

Proverbs 27:14

A person who flatters his neighbor
spreads a net for his feet.

Proverbs 29:5

Obedience

Listen, my son, to your father's instruction,
and don't reject your mother's teaching,

for they will be a garland of favor on your head
and pendants around your neck.

Proverbs 1:8-9

My son, don't forget my teaching,
but let your heart keep my commands;
for they will bring you
many days, a full life, and well-being.

Proverbs 3:1-2

Do not despise the LORD's instruction, my son,
and do not loathe his discipline;
for the LORD disciplines the one he loves,
just as a father disciplines the son in whom he delights.

Proverbs 3:11-12

Listen, sons, to a father's discipline,
and pay attention so that you may gain understanding,
for I am giving you good instruction.
Don't abandon my teaching.
When I was a son with my father,
tender and precious to my mother,
he taught me and said:
"Your heart must hold on to my words.
Keep my commands and live."

Proverbs 4:1-4

My son, pay attention to my words;
listen closely to my sayings.
Don't lose sight of them;
keep them within your heart.
For they are life to those who find them,
and health to one's whole body.

Proverbs 4:20-22

My son, pay attention to my wisdom;
listen closely to my understanding

so that you may maintain discretion
and your lips safeguard knowledge.

Proverbs 5:1-2

So now, sons, listen to me,
and don't turn away from the words from my mouth.
Keep your way far from her.
Don't go near the door of her house.
Otherwise, you will give up your vitality to others
and your years to someone cruel;
strangers will drain your resources,
and your hard-earned pay will end up in a foreigner's
house.

Proverbs 5:7-10

My son, keep your father's command,
and don't reject your mother's teaching.
Always bind them to your heart;
tie them around your neck.
When you walk here and there, they will guide you;
when you lie down, they will watch over you;
when you wake up, they will talk to you.

Proverbs 6:20-22

My son, obey my words,
and treasure my commands.
Keep my commands and live,
and guard my instructions
as you would the pupil of your eye.
Tie them to your fingers;
write them on the tablet of your heart.

Proverbs 7:1-3

A wise heart accepts commands,
but foolish lips will be destroyed.

Proverbs 10:8

A wise son responds to his father's discipline,
but a mocker doesn't listen to rebuke.

Proverbs 13:1

The one who has contempt for instruction will pay the penalty,
but the one who respects a command will be rewarded.

Proverbs 13:13

A fool despises his father's discipline,
but a person who accepts correction is sensible.

Proverbs 15:5

The one who keeps commands preserves himself;
one who disregards his ways will die.

Proverbs 19:16

Listen to your father who gave you life,
and don't despise your mother when she is old.

Proverbs 23:22

Those who reject the law praise the wicked,
but those who keep the law pit themselves against them.

Proverbs 28:4

A discerning son keeps the law,
but a companion of gluttons humiliates his father.

Proverbs 28:7

Oppression

The one who oppresses the poor person insults his Maker,
but one who is kind to the needy honors him.

Proverbs 14:31

All the days of the oppressed are miserable,
but a cheerful heart has a continual feast.

Proverbs 15:15

The one who mocks the poor insults his Maker,
and one who rejoices over calamity
will not go unpunished.

Proverbs 17:5

The one who shuts his ears to the cry of the poor
will himself also call out and not be answered.

Proverbs 21:13

Oppressing the poor to enrich oneself,
and giving to the rich—both lead only to poverty.

Proverbs 22:16

Don't rob a poor person because he is poor,
and don't crush the oppressed at the city gate,
for the LORD will champion their cause
and will plunder those who plunder them.

Proverbs 22:22-23

A destitute leader who oppresses the poor
is like a driving rain that leaves no food.

Proverbs 28:3

A leader who lacks understanding
is very oppressive,
but one who hates dishonest profit
prolongs his life.

Proverbs 28:16

The poor and the oppressor have this in common:
the LORD gives light to the eyes of both.

Proverbs 29:13

It is not for kings, Lemuel,
it is not for kings to drink wine
or for rulers to desire beer.
Otherwise, he will drink,
forget what is decreed,
and pervert justice for all the oppressed.

Proverbs 31:4-5

Speak up for those who have no voice,
for the justice of all who are dispossessed.
Speak up, judge righteously,
and defend the cause of the oppressed and needy.

Proverbs 31:8-9

Patience

A fool's displeasure is known at once,
but whoever ignores an insult is sensible.

Proverbs 12:16

A patient person shows great understanding,
but a quick-tempered one promotes foolishness.

Proverbs 14:29

Patience is better than power,
and controlling one's emotions, than capturing a city.

Proverbs 16:32

A person's insight gives him patience,
and his virtue is to overlook an offense.

Proverbs 19:11

A ruler can be persuaded through patience,
and a gentle tongue can break a bone.

Proverbs 25:15

Peace

Her ways [Wisdom's] are pleasant,
and all her paths, peaceful.

Proverbs 3:17

Deceit is in the hearts of those who plot evil,
but those who promote peace have joy.

Proverbs 12:20

A tranquil heart is life to the body,
but jealousy is rottenness to the bones.

Proverbs 14:30

A gentle answer turns away anger,
but a harsh word stirs up wrath.

Proverbs 15:1

A hot-tempered person stirs up conflict,
but one slow to anger calms strife.

Proverbs 15:18

When a person's ways please the LORD,
he makes even his enemies to be at peace with him.

Proverbs 16:7

Better a dry crust with peace
than a house full of feasting with strife.

Proverbs 17:1

Discipline your child, and it will bring you peace of mind
and give you delight.

Proverbs 29:17

Pride

The LORD hates six things;
in fact, seven are detestable to him:
arrogant eyes, a lying tongue,
hands that shed innocent blood,
a heart that plots wicked schemes,
feet eager to run to evil,
a lying witness who gives false testimony,
and one who stirs up trouble among brothers.

Proverbs 6:16-19

When arrogance comes, disgrace follows,
but with humility comes wisdom.

Proverbs 11:2

Arrogance leads to nothing but strife,
but wisdom is gained by those who take advice.

Proverbs 13:10

The LORD tears apart the house of the proud,
but he protects the widow's territory.

Proverbs 15:25

Everyone with a proud heart is detestable to the LORD;
be assured, he will not go unpunished.

Proverbs 16:5

Pride comes before destruction,
and an arrogant spirit before a fall.

Proverbs 16:18

Better to be lowly of spirit with the humble
than to divide plunder with the proud.

Proverbs 16:19

A fool does not delight in understanding,
but only wants to show off his opinions.

Proverbs 18:2

Before his downfall a person's heart is proud,
but humility comes before honor.

Proverbs 18:12

The lamp that guides the wicked—
haughty eyes and an arrogant heart—is sin.

Proverbs 21:4

The arrogant and proud person, named "Mocker,"
acts with excessive arrogance.

Proverbs 21:24

Don't gloat when your enemy falls,
and don't let your heart rejoice when he stumbles,
or the LORD will see, be displeased,
and turn his wrath away from him.

Proverbs 24:17-18

Don't boast about yourself before the king,
and don't stand in the place of the great;

for it is better for him to say to you, "Come up here!"
than to demote you in plain view of a noble.

Proverbs 25:6-7

The one who boasts about a gift that does not exist
is like clouds and wind without rain.

Proverbs 25:14

Do you see a person who is wise in his own eyes?
There is more hope for a fool than for him.

Proverbs 26:12

Don't boast about tomorrow,
for you don't know what a day might bring.

Proverbs 27:1

A servant pampered from his youth
will become arrogant later on.

Proverbs 29:21

A person's pride will humble him,
but a humble spirit will gain honor.

Proverbs 29:23

There is a generation that curses its father
and does not bless its mother.
There is a generation that is pure in its own eyes,
yet is not washed from its filth.
There is a generation—how haughty its eyes
and pretentious its looks.
There is a generation whose teeth are swords,
whose fangs are knives,
devouring the oppressed from the land
and the needy from among mankind.

Proverbs 30:11-14

Prosperity

He [the LORD] stores up success for the upright.

Proverbs 2:7a

Honor the LORD with your possessions
and with the first produce of your entire harvest;
then your barns will be completely filled,
and your vats will overflow with new wine.

Proverbs 3:9-10

I [Wisdom] love those who love me,
and those who search for me find me.
With me are riches and honor,
lasting wealth and righteousness.
My fruit is better than solid gold,
and my harvest than pure silver.
I walk in the ways of righteousness,
along the paths of justice,
giving wealth as an inheritance to those who love me,
and filling their treasuries.

Proverbs 8:17-21

One person gives freely,
yet gains more;

another withholds what is right,
only to become poor.

Proverbs 11:24

The one who works his land will have plenty of food,
but whoever chases fantasies lacks sense.

Proverbs 12:11

A person will be satisfied with good
by the fruit of his mouth,
and the work of a person's hands will reward him.

Proverbs 12:14

Wealth obtained by fraud will dwindle,
but whoever earns it through labor will multiply it.

Proverbs 13:11

Where there are no oxen, the feeding trough is empty,
but an abundant harvest comes through the strength of
an ox.

Proverbs 14:4

A poor person is hated even by his neighbor,
but there are many who love the rich.

Proverbs 14:20

There is profit in all hard work,
but endless talk leads only to poverty.

Proverbs 14:23

Plans fail when there is no counsel,
but with many advisers they succeed.

Proverbs 15:22

The one who understands a matter finds success,
and the one who trusts in the Lord will be happy.

Proverbs 16:20

One with a twisted mind will not succeed,
and one with deceitful speech will fall into ruin.

Proverbs 17:20

The one who acquires good sense loves himself;
one who safeguards understanding finds success.

Proverbs 19:8

The plans of the diligent certainly lead to profit,
but anyone who is reckless certainly becomes poor.

Proverbs 21:5

Know well the condition of your flock,
and pay attention to your herds,
for wealth is not forever;
not even a crown lasts for all time.
When hay is removed and new growth appears
and the grain from the hills is gathered in,
lambs will provide your clothing,
and goats, the price of a field;
there will be enough goat's milk for your food—
food for your household
and nourishment for your female servants.

Proverbs 27:23-27

A greedy person stirs up conflict,
but whoever trusts in the LORD will prosper.

Proverbs 28:25

Prudence

Let your eyes look forward;
fix your gaze straight ahead.
Carefully consider the path for your feet,
and all your ways will be established.
Don't turn to the right or to the left;
keep your feet away from evil.

Proverbs 4:25-27

The son who gathers during summer is prudent;
the son who sleeps during harvest is disgraceful.

Proverbs 10:5

When there are many words, sin is unavoidable,
but the one who controls his lips is prudent.

Proverbs 10:19

Whoever shows contempt for his neighbor lacks sense,
but a person with understanding keeps silent.

Proverbs 11:12

A shrewd person conceals knowledge,
but a foolish heart publicizes stupidity.

Proverbs 12:23

The inexperienced one believes anything,
but the sensible one watches his steps.

Proverbs 14:15

A wise person is cautious and turns from evil,
but a fool is easily angered and is careless.

Proverbs 14:16

A king favors a prudent servant,
but his anger falls on a disgraceful one.

Proverbs 14:35

For the prudent the path of life leads upward,
so that he may avoid going down to Sheol.

Proverbs 15:24

The mind of the righteous person thinks before answering,
but the mouth of the wicked blurts out evil things.

Proverbs 15:28

A prudent servant will rule over a disgraceful son
and share an inheritance among brothers.

Proverbs 17:2

Even zeal is not good without knowledge,
and the one who acts hastily sins.

Proverbs 19:2

A house and wealth are inherited from fathers,
but a prudent wife is from the LORD.

Proverbs 19:14

The person who strays from the way of prudence
will come to rest in the assembly of the departed spirits.

Proverbs 21:16

A wicked person puts on a bold face,
but the upright one considers his way.

Proverbs 21:29

A sensible person sees danger and takes cover,
but the inexperienced keep going and are punished.

Proverbs 22:3

Don't take a matter to court hastily.
Otherwise, what will you do afterward
if your opponent humiliates you?
Make your case with your opponent
without revealing another's secret;
otherwise, the one who hears will disgrace you,
and you'll never live it down.

Proverbs 25:8-10

A ruler can be persuaded through patience,
and a gentle tongue can break a bone.

Proverbs 25:15

A sensible person sees danger and takes cover;
the inexperienced keep going and are punished.

Proverbs 27:12

Purity

The LORD detests the plans of the one who is evil,
but pleasant words are pure.

Proverbs 15:26

Who can say, "I have kept my heart pure;
I am cleansed from my sin"?

Proverbs 20:9

Even a young man is known by his actions—
by whether his behavior is pure and upright.

Proverbs 20:11

A guilty one's conduct is crooked,
but the behavior of the innocent is upright.

Proverbs 21:8

The one who loves a pure heart
and gracious lips—the king is his friend.

Proverbs 22:11

Every word of God is pure;
he is a shield to those who take refuge in him.

Proverbs 30:5

There is a generation that is pure in its own eyes,
yet is not washed from its filth.

Proverbs 30:12

Righteousness

The LORD's curse is on the household of the wicked,
but he blesses the home of the righteous;

Proverbs 3:33

The path of the righteous is like the light of dawn,
shining brighter and brighter until midday.
But the way of the wicked is like the darkest gloom;
they don't know what makes them stumble.

Proverbs 4:18-19

Let your eyes look forward;
fix your gaze straight ahead.
Carefully consider the path for your feet,
and all your ways will be established.
Don't turn to the right or to the left;
keep your feet away from evil.

Proverbs 4:25-27

Ill-gotten gains do not profit anyone,
but righteousness rescues from death.

Proverbs 10:2

Blessings are on the head of the righteous,
but the mouth of the wicked conceals violence.

Proverbs 10:6

The remembrance of the righteous is a blessing,
but the name of the wicked will rot.

Proverbs 10:7

The mouth of the righteous is a fountain of life,
but the mouth of the wicked conceals violence.

Proverbs 10:11

The reward of the righteous is life;
the wages of the wicked is punishment.

Proverbs 10:16

The lips of the righteous feed many,
but fools die for lack of sense.

Proverbs 10:21

What the wicked dreads will come to him,
but what the righteous desire will be given to them.

Proverbs 10:24

When the whirlwind passes,
the wicked are no more,
but the righteous are secure forever.

Proverbs 10:25

The hope of the righteous is joy,
but the expectation of the wicked will perish.

Proverbs 10:28

The righteous will never be shaken,
but the wicked will not remain on the earth.

Proverbs 10:30

The mouth of the righteous produces wisdom,
but a perverse tongue will be cut out.

Proverbs 10:31

The lips of the righteous know what is appropriate,
but the mouth of the wicked, only what is perverse.

Proverbs 10:32

The integrity of the upright guides them,
but the perversity of the treacherous destroys them.

Proverbs 11:3

Wealth is not profitable on a day of wrath,
but righteousness rescues from death.

Proverbs 11:4

The righteousness of the blameless clears his path,
but the wicked person will fall because of his wickedness.

Proverbs 11:5

The righteousness of the upright rescues them,
but the treacherous are trapped by their own desires.

Proverbs 11:6

The righteous one is rescued from trouble;
in his place, the wicked one goes in.

Proverbs 11:8

When the righteous thrive, a city rejoices;
when the wicked die, there is joyful shouting.

Proverbs 11:10

A city is built up by the blessing of the upright,
but it is torn down by the mouth of the wicked.

Proverbs 11:11

The wicked person earns an empty wage,
but the one who sows righteousness, a true reward.

Proverbs 11:18

Genuine righteousness leads to life,
but pursuing evil leads to death.

Proverbs 11:19

Those with twisted minds are detestable to the Lord,
but those with blameless conduct are his delight.

Proverbs 11:20

Be assured that a wicked person
will not go unpunished,
but the offspring of the righteous will escape.

Proverbs 11:21

The desire of the righteous turns out well,
but the hope of the wicked leads to wrath.

Proverbs 11:23

Anyone trusting in his riches will fall,
but the righteous will flourish like foliage.

Proverbs 11:28

The fruit of the righteous is a tree of life,
and a wise person captivates people.

Proverbs 11:30

If the righteous will be repaid on earth,
how much more the wicked and sinful.

Proverbs 11:31

One who is good obtains favor from the LORD,
but he condemns a person who schemes.

Proverbs 12:2

No one can be made secure by wickedness,
but the root of the righteous is immovable.

Proverbs 12:3

The thoughts of the righteous are just,
but guidance from the wicked is deceitful.

Proverbs 12:5

The words of the wicked are a deadly ambush,
but the speech of the upright rescues them.

Proverbs 12:6

The wicked are overthrown and perish,
but the house of the righteous will stand.

Proverbs 12:7

The righteous cares about his animal's health,
but even the merciful acts of the wicked are cruel.

Proverbs 12:10

The wicked desire what evil people have caught,
but the root of the righteous is productive.

Proverbs 12:12

By rebellious speech an evil person is trapped,
but a righteous person escapes from trouble.

Proverbs 12:13

No disaster overcomes the righteous,
but the wicked are full of misery.

Proverbs 12:21

A righteous person is careful in dealing with his neighbor,
but the ways of the wicked lead them astray.

Proverbs 12:26

There is life in the path of righteousness,
and in its path there is no death.

Proverbs 12:28

The righteous hate lying,
but the wicked bring disgust and shame.

Proverbs 13:5

Righteousness guards people of integrity,
but wickedness undermines the sinner.

Proverbs 13:6

The light of the righteous shines brightly,
but the lamp of the wicked is put out.

Proverbs 13:9

Disaster pursues sinners,
but good rewards the righteous.

Proverbs 13:21

A good man leaves an inheritance to his grandchildren,
but the sinner's wealth is stored up for the righteous.

Proverbs 13:22

A righteous person eats until he is satisfied,
but the stomach of the wicked is empty.

Proverbs 13:25

The house of the wicked will be destroyed,
but the tent of the upright will flourish.

Proverbs 14:11

The evil bow before those who are good,
and the wicked, at the gates of the righteous.

Proverbs 14:19

Don't those who plan evil go astray?
But those who plan good find loyalty and faithfulness.

Proverbs 14:22

The wicked one is thrown down by his own sin,
but the righteous one has a refuge in his death.

Proverbs 14:32

Righteousness exalts a nation,
but sin is a disgrace to any people.

Proverbs 14:34

The house of the righteous has great wealth,
but trouble accompanies the income of the wicked.

Proverbs 15:6

The sacrifice of the wicked is detestable to the LORD,
but the prayer of the upright is his delight.

Proverbs 15:8

The LORD detests the way of the wicked,
but he loves the one who pursues righteousness.

Proverbs 15:9

A slacker's way is like a thorny hedge,
but the path of the upright is a highway.

Proverbs 15:19

The mind of the righteous person thinks before answering,
but the mouth of the wicked blurts out evil things.

Proverbs 15:28

The LORD is far from the wicked,
but he hears the prayer of the righteous.

Proverbs 15:29

Better a little with righteousness
than great income with injustice.

Proverbs 16:8

Wicked behavior is detestable to kings,
since a throne is established through righteousness.

Proverbs 16:12

Righteous lips are a king's delight,
and he loves one who speaks honestly.

Proverbs 16:13

The highway of the upright avoids evil;
the one who guards his way protects his life.

Proverbs 16:17

Gray hair is a glorious crown;
it is found in the ways of righteousness.

Proverbs 16:31

The name of the LORD is a strong tower;
the righteous run to it and are protected.

Proverbs 18:10

A righteous person acts with integrity;
his children who come after him will be happy.

Proverbs 20:7

Doing what is righteous and just
is more acceptable to the LORD than sacrifice.

Proverbs 21:3

A guilty one's conduct is crooked,
but the behavior of the innocent is upright.

Proverbs 21:8

The wicked are a ransom for the righteous,
and the treacherous, for the upright.

Proverbs 21:18

The one who pursues righteousness and faithful love
will find life, righteousness, and honor.

Proverbs 21:21

A slacker's craving will kill him
because his hands refuse to work.
He is filled with craving all day long,
but the righteous give and don't hold back.

Proverbs 21:25-26

A wicked person puts on a bold face,
but the upright one considers his way.

Proverbs 21:29

The father of a righteous son will rejoice greatly,
and one who fathers a wise son will delight in him.
Let your father and mother have joy,
and let her who gave birth to you rejoice.

Proverbs 23:24-25

Don't set an ambush, you wicked one,
at the camp of the righteous man;
don't destroy his dwelling.
Though a righteous person falls seven times,
he will get up,
but the wicked will stumble into ruin.

Proverbs 24:15-16

The wicked flee when no one is pursuing them,
but the righteous are as bold as a lion.

Proverbs 28:1

Those who reject the law praise the wicked,
but those who keep the law pit themselves against them.

Proverbs 28:4

When the righteous triumph,
there is great rejoicing,
but when the wicked come to power,
people hide.

Proverbs 28:12

When the righteous flourish, the people rejoice,
but when the wicked rule, people groan.

Proverbs 29:2

An evil person is caught by sin,
but the righteous one sings and rejoices.

Proverbs 29:6

The righteous person knows the rights of the poor,
but the wicked one does not understand these concerns.

Proverbs 29:7

When the wicked increase, rebellion increases,
but the righteous will see their downfall.

Proverbs 29:16

An unjust person is detestable to the righteous,
and one whose way is upright
is detestable to the wicked.

Proverbs 29:27

Rulers

It is by me [Wisdom] that kings reign
and rulers enact just law;
by me, princes lead,
as do nobles and all righteous judges.

Proverbs 8:15-16

When the righteous thrive, a city rejoices;
when the wicked die, there is joyful shouting.

Proverbs 11:10

A large population is a king's splendor,
but a shortage of people is a ruler's devastation.

Proverbs 14:28

A king favors a prudent servant,
but his anger falls on a disgraceful one.

Proverbs 14:35

God's verdict is on the lips of a king;
his mouth should not give an unfair judgment.

Proverbs 16:10

Wicked behavior is detestable to kings,
since a throne is established through righteousness.

Proverbs 16:12

Righteous lips are a king's delight,
and he loves one who speaks honestly.

Proverbs 16:13

A king's fury is a messenger of death,
but a wise person appeases it.

Proverbs 16:14

When a king's face lights up, there is life;
his favor is like a cloud with spring rain.

Proverbs 16:15

Eloquent words are not appropriate on a fool's lips;
how much worse are lies for a ruler.

Proverbs 17:7

Many seek a ruler's favor,
and everyone is a friend of one who gives gifts.

Proverbs 19:6

Luxury is not appropriate for a fool—
how much less for a slave to rule over princes!

Proverbs 19:10

A king's rage is like the roaring of a lion,
but his favor is like dew on the grass.

Proverbs 19:12

A king's terrible wrath is like the roaring of a lion;
anyone who provokes him endangers himself.

Proverbs 20:2

A king sitting on a throne to judge
separates out all evil with his eyes.

Proverbs 20:8

A wise king separates out the wicked
and drives the threshing wheel over them.

Proverbs 20:26

Loyalty and faithfulness guard a king;
through loyalty he maintains his throne.

Proverbs 20:28

A king's heart is like channeled water in the LORD's
hand:
He directs it wherever he chooses.

Proverbs 21:1

The one who loves a pure heart
and gracious lips—the king is his friend.

Proverbs 22:11

Do you see a person skilled in his work?
He will stand in the presence of kings.
He will not stand in the presence of the unknown.

Proverbs 22:29

My son, fear the LORD, as well as the king,
and don't associate with rebels,
for destruction will come suddenly from them;
who knows what distress these two can bring?

Proverbs 24:21-22

As the heavens are high and the earth is deep,
so the hearts of kings cannot be investigated.

Proverbs 25:3

Remove impurities from silver,
and material will be produced for a silversmith.
Remove the wicked from the king's presence,
and his throne will be established in righteousness.

Proverbs 25:4-5

Don't boast about yourself before the king,
and don't stand in the place of the great;
for it is better for him to say to you, "Come up here!"
than to demote you in plain view of a noble.

Proverbs 25:6-7

A ruler can be persuaded through patience,
and a gentle tongue can break a bone.

Proverbs 25:15

Good news from a distant land
is like cold water to a parched throat.

Proverbs 25:25

When a land is in rebellion, it has many rulers,
but with a discerning and knowledgeable person, it
endures.

Proverbs 28:2

A destitute leader who oppresses the poor
is like a driving rain that leaves no food.

Proverbs 28:3

When the righteous triumph,
there is great rejoicing,
but when the wicked come to power,
people hide.

Proverbs 28:12

A wicked ruler over a helpless people
is like a roaring lion or a charging bear.

Proverbs 28:15

A leader who lacks understanding
is very oppressive,
but one who hates dishonest profit
prolongs his life.

Proverbs 28:16

When the wicked come to power,
people hide,
but when they are destroyed,
the righteous flourish.

Proverbs 28:28

When the righteous flourish, the people rejoice,
but when the wicked rule, people groan.

Proverbs 29:2

By justice a king brings stability to a land,
but a person who demands "contributions"
demolishes it.

Proverbs 29:4

If a ruler listens to lies,
all his officials will be wicked.

Proverbs 29:12

A king who judges the poor with fairness—
his throne will be established forever.

Proverbs 29:14

Many desire a ruler's favor,
but a person receives justice from the LORD.

Proverbs 29:26

The words of King Lemuel,
a pronouncement that his mother taught him:
What should I say, my son?
What, son of my womb?
What, son of my vows?
Don't spend your energy on women
or your efforts on those who destroy kings.
It is not for kings, Lemuel,
it is not for kings to drink wine
or for rulers to desire beer.
Otherwise, he will drink,
forget what is decreed,
and pervert justice for all the oppressed.
Give beer to one who is dying
and wine to one whose life is bitter.
Let him drink so that he can forget his poverty
and remember his trouble no more.
Speak up for those who have no voice,
for the justice of all who are dispossessed.
Speak up, judge righteously,
and defend the cause of the oppressed and needy.

Proverbs 31:1-9

Security

But whoever listens to me [Wisdom] will live securely
and be undisturbed by the dread of danger.

Proverbs 1:33

Discretion will watch over you,
and understanding will guard you.

Proverbs 2:11

Maintain sound wisdom and discretion.
My son, don't lose sight of them.
They will be life for you
and adornment for your neck.
Then you will go safely on your way;
your foot will not stumble.
When you lie down, you will not be afraid;
you will lie down, and your sleep will be pleasant.

Proverbs 3:21-24

Don't fear sudden danger
or the ruin of the wicked when it comes,
for the LORD will be your confidence
and will keep your foot from a snare.

Proverbs 3:25-26

Don't abandon wisdom, and she will watch over you;
love her, and she will guard you.

Proverbs 4:6

The one who lives with integrity lives securely,
but whoever perverts his ways will be found out.

Proverbs 10:9

When the whirlwind passes,
the wicked are no more,
but the righteous are secure forever.

Proverbs 10:25

The way of the LORD is a stronghold for the honorable,
but destruction awaits the malicious.

Proverbs 10:29

The righteous will never be shaken,
but the wicked will not remain on the earth.

Proverbs 10:30

No one can be made secure by wickedness,
but the root of the righteous is immovable.

Proverbs 12:3

The proud speech of a fool brings a rod of discipline,
but the lips of the wise protect them.

Proverbs 14:3

In the fear of the LORD one has strong confidence
and his children have a refuge.

Proverbs 14:26

The wicked one is thrown down by his own sin,
but the righteous one has a refuge in his death.

Proverbs 14:32

The fear of the LORD leads to life;
one will sleep at night without danger.

Proverbs 19:23

The one who trusts in himself is a fool,
but one who walks in wisdom will be safe.

Proverbs 28:26

The fear of mankind is a snare,
but the one who trusts in the Lord is protected.

Proverbs 29:25

Self-control

When there are many words, sin is unavoidable,
but the one who controls his lips is prudent.

Proverbs 10:19

Whoever shows contempt for his neighbor lacks sense,
but a person with understanding keeps silent.

Proverbs 11:12

The one who guards his mouth protects his life;
the one who opens his lips invites his own ruin.

Proverbs 13:3

Patience is better than power,
and controlling one's emotions, than capturing a city.

Proverbs 16:32

The one who has knowledge restrains his words,
and one who keeps a cool head
is a person of understanding.

Proverbs 17:27

The one who guards his mouth and tongue
keeps himself out of trouble.

Proverbs 21:23

A person who does not control his temper
is like a city whose wall is broken down.

Proverbs 25:28

A fool gives full vent to his anger,
but a wise person holds it in check.

Proverbs 29:11

Sovereignty of God

Trust in the LORD with all your heart,
and do not rely on your own understanding;
in all your ways know him,
and he will make your paths straight.

Proverbs 3:5-6

Don't fear sudden danger
or the ruin of the wicked when it comes,

for the LORD will be your confidence
and will keep your foot from a snare.

Proverbs 3:25-26

For a man's ways are before the LORD's eyes,
and he considers all his paths.

Proverbs 5:21

The LORD's blessing enriches,
and he adds no painful effort to it.

Proverbs 10:22

The eyes of the LORD are everywhere,
observing the wicked and the good.

Proverbs 15:3

Sheol and Abaddon lie open before the LORD—
how much more, human hearts.

Proverbs 15:11

The LORD tears apart the house of the proud,
but he protects the widow's territory.

Proverbs 15:25

The reflections of the heart belong to mankind,
but the answer of the tongue is from the LORD.

Proverbs 16:1

All a person's ways seem right to him,
but the LORD weighs motives.

Proverbs 16:2

Commit your activities to the LORD,
and your plans will be established.

Proverbs 16:3

The LORD has prepared everything for his purpose—
even the wicked for the day of disaster.

Proverbs 16:4

A person's heart plans his way,
but the LORD determines his steps.

Proverbs 16:9

The lot is cast into the lap,
but its every decision is from the LORD.

Proverbs 16:33

Many plans are in a person's heart,
but the LORD's decree will prevail.

Proverbs 19:21

Don't say, "I will avenge this evil!"
Wait on the LORD, and he will rescue you.

Proverbs 20:22

Even a courageous person's steps are determined by the
LORD,
so how can anyone understand his own way?

Proverbs 20:24

The LORD's lamp sheds light on a person's life,
searching the innermost parts.

Proverbs 20:27

A king's heart is like channeled water in the LORD's
hand:
He directs it wherever he chooses.

Proverbs 21:1

The Righteous One considers the house of the wicked;
he brings the wicked to ruin.

Proverbs 21:12

No wisdom, no understanding, and no counsel
will prevail against the LORD.

Proverbs 21:30

A horse is prepared for the day of battle,
but victory comes from the LORD.

Proverbs 21:31

The LORD's eyes keep watch over knowledge,
but he overthrows the words of the treacherous.

Proverbs 22:12

The poor and the oppressor have this in common:
the LORD gives light to the eyes of both.

Proverbs 29:13

The fear of mankind is a snare,
but the one who trusts in the LORD is protected.

Proverbs 29:25

Many desire a ruler's favor,
but a person receives justice from the LORD.

Proverbs 29:26

Who has gone up to heaven and come down?
Who has gathered the wind in his hands?
Who has bound up the waters in a cloak?
Who has established all the ends of the earth?
What is his name,
and what is the name of his son—
if you know?

Proverbs 30:4

Sowing & Reaping

Since I [Wisdom] called out and you refused,
extended my hand and no one paid attention,
since you neglected all my counsel

and did not accept my correction,
I, in turn, will laugh at your calamity.
I will mock when terror strikes you,
when terror strikes you like a storm
and your calamity comes like a whirlwind,
when trouble and stress overcome you.

Proverbs 1:24-27

Because they hated knowledge,
didn't choose to fear the LORD,
were not interested in my counsel,
and rejected all my correction,
they will eat the fruit of their way
and be glutted with their own schemes.
For the apostasy of the inexperienced will kill them,
and the complacency of fools will destroy them.
But whoever listens to me [Wisdom] will live securely
and be undisturbed by the dread of danger.

Proverbs 1:29-33

For the upright will inhabit the land,
and those of integrity will remain in it;
but the wicked will be cut off from the land,
and the treacherous ripped out of it.

Proverbs 2:21-22

My son, don't forget my teaching,
but let your heart keep my commands;
for they will bring you
many days, a full life, and well-being.

Proverbs 3:1-2

Honor the LORD with your possessions
and with the first produce of your entire harvest;
then your barns will be completely filled,
and your vats will overflow with new wine.

Proverbs 3:9-10

The LORD's curse is on the household of the wicked,
but he blesses the home of the righteous;
He mocks those who mock,
but gives grace to the humble.
The wise will inherit honor,
but he holds up fools to dishonor.

Proverbs 3:33-35

So now, sons, listen to me,
and don't turn away from the words from my mouth.
Keep your way far from her.
Don't go near the door of her house.
Otherwise, you will give up your vitality to others
and your years to someone cruel;
strangers will drain your resources,
and your hard-earned pay will end up in a foreigner's
house.

Proverbs 5:7-10

A wicked man's iniquities will trap him;
he will become tangled in the ropes of his own sin.
He will die because there is no discipline,
and be lost because of his great stupidity.

Proverbs 5:22-23

He always plots evil with perversity in his heart;
he stirs up trouble.
Therefore calamity will strike him suddenly;
he will be shattered instantly, beyond recovery.

Proverbs 6:14-15

Can a man embrace fire
and his clothes not be burned?
Can a man walk on burning coals
without scorching his feet?
So it is with the one who sleeps with
another man's wife;

no one who touches her will go unpunished.
People don't despise the thief if he steals
to satisfy himself when he is hungry.
Still, if caught, he must pay seven times as much;
he must give up all the wealth in his house.
The one who commits adultery lacks sense;
whoever does so destroys himself.
He will get a beating and dishonor,
and his disgrace will never be removed.
For jealousy enrages a husband,
and he will show no mercy when he takes revenge.
He will not be appeased by anything
or be persuaded by lavish bribes.

Proverbs 6:27-35

I [Wisdom] love those who love me,
and those who search for me find me.
With me are riches and honor,
lasting wealth and righteousness.
My fruit is better than solid gold,
and my harvest than pure silver.
I walk in the ways of righteousness,
along the paths of justice,
giving wealth as an inheritance to those who love me,
and filling their treasuries.

Proverbs 8:17-21

For the one who finds me [Wisdom] finds life
and obtains favor from the LORD,
but the one who misses me harms himself;
all who hate me love death.

Proverbs 8:35-36

If you are wise, you are wise for your own benefit;
if you mock, you alone will bear the consequences.

Proverbs 9:12

The LORD will not let the righteous go hungry,
but he denies the wicked what they crave.

Proverbs 10:3

The one who lives with integrity lives securely,
but whoever perverts his ways will be found out.

Proverbs 10:9

The reward of the righteous is life;
the wages of the wicked is punishment.

Proverbs 10:16

What the wicked dreads will come to him,
but what the righteous desire will be given to them.

Proverbs 10:24

When the whirlwind passes,
the wicked are no more,
but the righteous are secure forever.

Proverbs 10:25

The fear of the LORD prolongs life,
but the years of the wicked are cut short.

Proverbs 10:27

The hope of the righteous is joy,
but the expectation of the wicked will perish.

Proverbs 10:28

The way of the LORD is a stronghold for the honorable,
but destruction awaits the malicious.

Proverbs 10:29

The righteous will never be shaken,
but the wicked will not remain on the earth.

Proverbs 10:30

The integrity of the upright guides them,
but the perversity of the treacherous destroys them.

Proverbs 11:3

The righteousness of the blameless clears his path,
but the wicked person will fall because of his wickedness.
Proverbs 11:5

The righteousness of the upright rescues them,
but the treacherous are trapped by their own desires.
Proverbs 11:6

The righteous one is rescued from trouble;
in his place, the wicked one goes in.
Proverbs 11:8

A kind man benefits himself,
but a cruel person brings ruin on himself.
Proverbs 11:17

The wicked person earns an empty wage,
but the one who sows righteousness, a true reward.
Proverbs 11:18

Genuine righteousness leads to life,
but pursuing evil leads to death.
Proverbs 11:19

Be assured that a wicked person
will not go unpunished,
but the offspring of the righteous will escape.
Proverbs 11:21

The desire of the righteous turns out well,
but the hope of the wicked leads to wrath.
Proverbs 11:23

One person gives freely,
yet gains more;
another withholds what is right,
only to become poor.

Proverbs 11:24

A generous person will be enriched,
and the one who gives a drink of water
will receive water.

Proverbs 11:25

People will curse anyone who hoards grain,
but a blessing will come to the one who sells it.

Proverbs 11:26

The one who searches for what is good seeks favor,
but if someone looks for trouble, it will come to him.

Proverbs 11:27

Anyone trusting in his riches will fall,
but the righteous will flourish like foliage.

Proverbs 11:28

The one who brings ruin on his household
will inherit the wind,
and a fool will be a slave
to someone whose heart is wise.

Proverbs 11:29

If the righteous will be repaid on earth,
how much more the wicked and sinful.

Proverbs 11:31

The wicked are overthrown and perish,
but the house of the righteous will stand.

Proverbs 12:7

The one who works his land will have plenty of food,
but whoever chases fantasies lacks sense.

Proverbs 12:11

A person will be satisfied with good
by the fruit of his mouth,
and the work of a person's hands will reward him.

Proverbs 12:14

No disaster overcomes the righteous,
but the wicked are full of misery.

Proverbs 12:21

The one who guards his mouth protects his life;
the one who opens his lips invites his own ruin.

Proverbs 13:3

The slacker craves, yet has nothing,
but the diligent is fully satisfied.

Proverbs 13:4

Wealth obtained by fraud will dwindle,
but whoever earns it through labor will multiply it.

Proverbs 13:11

The one who has contempt for instruction will pay the
penalty,
but the one who respects a command will be rewarded.

Proverbs 13:13

A wicked envoy falls into trouble,
but a trustworthy courier brings healing.

Proverbs 13:17

Disaster pursues sinners,
but good rewards the righteous.

Proverbs 13:21

A good man leaves an inheritance to his grandchildren,
but the sinner's wealth is stored up for the righteous.

Proverbs 13:22

A righteous person eats until he is satisfied,
but the stomach of the wicked is empty.

Proverbs 13:25

The house of the wicked will be destroyed,
but the tent of the upright will flourish.

Proverbs 14:11

The disloyal one will get what his conduct deserves,
and a good one, what his deeds deserve.

Proverbs 14:14

Don't those who plan evil go astray?
But those who plan good find loyalty and faithfulness.

Proverbs 14:22

The wicked one is thrown down by his own sin,
but the righteous one has a refuge in his death.

Proverbs 14:32

The house of the righteous has great wealth,
but trouble accompanies the income of the wicked.

Proverbs 15:6

The one who profits dishonestly troubles his household,
but the one who hates bribes will live.

Proverbs 15:27

The one who mocks the poor insults his Maker,
and one who rejoices over calamity
will not go unpunished.

Proverbs 17:5

If anyone returns evil for good,
evil will never depart from his house.

Proverbs 17:13

One with a twisted mind will not succeed,
and one with deceitful speech will fall into ruin.

Proverbs 17:20

A false witness will not go unpunished,
and one who utters lies will not escape.

Proverbs 19:5

A false witness will not go unpunished,
and one who utters lies perishes.

Proverbs 19:9

Kindness to the poor is a loan to the LORD,
and he will give a reward to the lender.

Proverbs 19:17

Food gained by fraud is sweet to a person,
but afterward his mouth is full of gravel.

Proverbs 20:17

The one who shuts his ears to the cry of the poor
will himself also call out and not be answered.

Proverbs 21:13

There are thorns and snares on the way of the crooked;
the one who guards himself stays far from them.

Proverbs 22:5

The one who sows injustice will reap disaster,
and the rod of his fury will be destroyed.

Proverbs 22:8

Don't rob a poor person because he is poor,
and don't crush the oppressed at the city gate,
for the LORD will champion their cause
and will plunder those who plunder them.

Proverbs 22:22-23

If you do nothing in a difficult time,
your strength is limited.
Rescue those being taken off to death,
and save those stumbling toward slaughter.
If you say, "But we didn't know about this,"
won't he who weighs hearts consider it?
Won't he who protects your life know?
Won't he repay a person according to his work?

Proverbs 24:10-12

Don't set an ambush, you wicked one,
at the camp of the righteous man;
don't destroy his dwelling.
Though a righteous person falls seven times,
he will get up,
but the wicked will stumble into ruin.

Proverbs 24:15-16

Don't be agitated by evildoers,
and don't envy the wicked.
For the evil have no future;
the lamp of the wicked will be put out.

Proverbs 24:19-20

The one who digs a pit will fall into it,
and whoever rolls a stone—
it will come back on him.

Proverbs 26:27

Whoever tends a fig tree will eat its fruit,
and whoever looks after his master will be honored.

Proverbs 27:18

Whoever increases his wealth through excessive interest
collects it for one who is kind to the poor.

Proverbs 28:8

The one who leads the upright into an evil way
will fall into his own pit,
but the blameless will inherit what is good.

Proverbs 28:10

The one who lives with integrity will be helped,
but one who distorts right and wrong
will suddenly fall.

Proverbs 28:18

The one who works his land
will have plenty of food,
but whoever chases fantasies
will have his fill of poverty.

Proverbs 28:19

The one who gives to the poor
will not be in need,
but one who turns his eyes away
will receive many curses.

Proverbs 28:27

As for the eye that ridicules a father
and despises obedience to a mother,
may ravens of the valley pluck it out
and young vultures eat it.

Proverbs 30:17

Speech

Don't let your mouth speak dishonestly,
and don't let your lips talk deviously.

Proverbs 4:2

She seduces him with her persistent pleading;
she lures with her flattering talk.

Proverbs 7:21

Listen, for I [Wisdom] speak of noble things,
and what my lips say is right.
For my mouth tells the truth,
and wickedness is detestable to my lips.
All the words from my mouth are righteous;
none of them are deceptive or perverse.
All of them are clear to the perceptive,
and right to those who discover knowledge.

Proverbs 8:6-9

Blessings are on the head of the righteous,
but the mouth of the wicked conceals violence.

Proverbs 10:6

A wise heart accepts commands,
but foolish lips will be destroyed.

Proverbs 10:8

A sly wink of the eye causes grief,
and foolish lips will be destroyed.

Proverbs 10:10

The mouth of the righteous is a fountain of life,
but the mouth of the wicked conceals violence.

Proverbs 10:11

Wisdom is found on the lips of the discerning,
but a rod is for the back of the one who lacks sense.

Proverbs 10:13

The wise store up knowledge,
but the mouth of the fool hastens destruction.

Proverbs 10:14

The one who conceals hatred has lying lips,
and whoever spreads slander is a fool.

Proverbs 10:18

When there are many words, sin is unavoidable,
but the one who controls his lips is prudent.

Proverbs 10:19

The tongue of the righteous is pure silver;
the heart of the wicked is of little value.

Proverbs 10:20

The lips of the righteous feed many,
but fools die for lack of sense.

Proverbs 10:21

The mouth of the righteous produces wisdom,
but a perverse tongue will be cut out.

Proverbs 10:31

The lips of the righteous know what is appropriate,
but the mouth of the wicked, only what is perverse.

Proverbs 10:32

With his mouth the ungodly destroys his neighbor,
but through knowledge the righteous are rescued.

Proverbs 11:9

A city is built up by the blessing of the upright,
but it is torn down by the mouth of the wicked.

Proverbs 11:11

The words of the wicked are a deadly ambush,
but the speech of the upright rescues them.

Proverbs 12:6

By rebellious speech an evil person is trapped,
but a righteous person escapes from trouble.

Proverbs 12:13

A person will be satisfied with good
by the fruit of his mouth,
and the work of a person's hands will reward him.

Proverbs 12:14

Whoever speaks the truth declares what is right,
but a false witness speaks deceit.

Proverbs 12:17

There is one who speaks rashly,
like a piercing sword;
but the tongue of the wise brings healing.

Proverbs 12:18

Truthful lips endure forever,
but a lying tongue, only a moment.

Proverbs 12:19

Lying lips are detestable to the LORD,
but faithful people are his delight.

Proverbs 12:22

Anxiety in a person's heart weighs it down,
but a good word cheers it up.

Proverbs 12:25

From the fruit of his mouth,
a person will enjoy good things,
but treacherous people have an appetite for violence.

Proverbs 13:2

The one who guards his mouth protects his life;
the one who opens his lips invites his own ruin.

Proverbs 13:3

The proud speech of a fool brings a rod of discipline,
but the lips of the wise protect them.

Proverbs 14:3

Stay away from a foolish person;
you will gain no knowledge from his speech.

Proverbs 14:7

There is profit in all hard work,
but endless talk leads only to poverty.

Proverbs 14:23

A gentle answer turns away anger,
but a harsh word stirs up wrath.

Proverbs 15:1

The tongue of the wise makes knowledge attractive,
but the mouth of fools blurts out foolishness.

Proverbs 15:2

The tongue that heals is a tree of life,
but a devious tongue breaks the spirit.

Proverbs 15:4

The lips of the wise broadcast knowledge,
but not so the heart of fools.

Proverbs 15:7

A discerning mind seeks knowledge,
but the mouth of fools feeds on foolishness.

Proverbs 15:14

A person takes joy in giving an answer;
and a timely word—how good that is!

Proverbs 15:23

The LORD detests the plans of the one who is evil,
but pleasant words are pure.

Proverbs 15:26

The mind of the righteous person thinks before answering,
but the mouth of the wicked blurts out evil things.

Proverbs 15:28

The reflections of the heart belong to mankind,
but the answer of the tongue is from the LORD.

Proverbs 16:1

Righteous lips are a king's delight,
and he loves one who speaks honestly.

Proverbs 16:13

Anyone with a wise heart is called discerning,
and pleasant speech increases learning.

Proverbs 16:21

The heart of a wise person instructs his mouth;
it adds learning to his speech.

Proverbs 16:23

Pleasant words are a honeycomb:
sweet to the taste and health to the body.

Proverbs 16:24

A worthless person digs up evil,
and his speech is like a scorching fire.

Proverbs 16:27

A wicked person listens to malicious talk;
a liar pays attention to a destructive tongue.

Proverbs 17:4

Eloquent words are not appropriate on a fool's lips;
how much worse are lies for a ruler.

Proverbs 17:7

The one who has knowledge restrains his words,
and one who keeps a cool head
is a person of understanding.

Proverbs 17:27

Even a fool is considered wise when he keeps silent—
discerning, when he seals his lips.

Proverbs 17:28

The words of a person's mouth are deep waters,
a flowing river, a fountain of wisdom.

Proverbs 18:4

A fool's lips lead to strife,
and his mouth provokes a beating.

Proverbs 18:6

A fool's mouth is his devastation,
and his lips are a trap for his life.

Proverbs 18:7

A gossip's words are like choice food
that goes down to one's innermost being.

Proverbs 18:8

From the fruit of a person's mouth his stomach is satisfied;
he is filled with the product of his lips.

Proverbs 18:20

Death and life are in the power of the tongue,
and those who love it will eat its fruit.

Proverbs 18:21

There is gold and a multitude of jewels,
but knowledgeable lips are a rare treasure.

Proverbs 20:15

The one who reveals secrets is a constant gossip;
avoid someone with a big mouth.

Proverbs 20:19

The one who guards his mouth and tongue
keeps himself out of trouble.

Proverbs 21:23

The LORD's eyes keep watch over knowledge,
but he overthrows the words of the treacherous.

Proverbs 22:12

The mouth of the forbidden woman is a deep pit;
a man cursed by the LORD will fall into it.

Proverbs 22:14

Listen closely, pay attention to the words of the wise,
and apply your mind to my knowledge.
For it is pleasing if you keep them within you
and if they are constantly on your lips.

Proverbs 22:17-18

My son, if your heart is wise,
my heart will indeed rejoice.
My innermost being will celebrate
when your lips say what is right.

Proverbs 23:15-16

A ruler can be persuaded through patience,
and a gentle tongue can break a bone.

Proverbs 25:15

The north wind produces rain,
and a backbiting tongue, angry looks.

Proverbs 25:23

A gossip's words are like choice food
that goes down to one's innermost being.

Proverbs 26:22

Smooth lips with an evil heart
are like glaze on an earthen vessel.

Proverbs 26:23

A hateful person disguises himself with his speech
and harbors deceit within.
When he speaks graciously, don't believe him,
for there are seven detestable things in his heart.
Though his hatred is concealed by deception,
his evil will be revealed in the assembly.

Proverbs 26:24-26

A lying tongue hates those it crushes,
and a flattering mouth causes ruin.

Proverbs 26:28

Let another praise you, and not your own mouth—
a stranger, and not your own lips.

Proverbs 27:2

One who rebukes a person will later find more favor
than one who flatters with his tongue.

Proverbs 28:23

A person who flatters his neighbor
spreads a net for his feet.

Proverbs 29:5

A servant cannot be disciplined by words;
though he understands, he doesn't respond.

Proverbs 29:19

Every word of God is pure;
he is a shield to those who take refuge in him.
Don't add to his words,
or he will rebuke you, and you will be proved a liar.

Proverbs 30:5-6

Two things I ask of you;
don't deny them to me before I die:
Keep falsehood and deceitful words far from me.

Proverbs 30:7-8a

Her mouth speaks wisdom,
and loving instruction is on her tongue.

Proverbs 31:26

Temptation

My son, if sinners entice you,
don't be persuaded.
If they say—"Come with us!
Let's set an ambush and kill someone.
Let's attack some innocent person just for fun!
Let's swallow them alive, like Sheol,
whole, like those who go down to the Pit.
We'll find all kinds of valuable property
and fill our houses with plunder.

Throw in your lot with us,
and we'll all share the loot"—
my son, don't travel that road with them
or set foot on their path,
because their feet run toward evil
and they hurry to shed blood.

Proverbs 1:10-16

Though the lips of the forbidden woman drip honey
and her words are smoother than oil,
in the end she's as bitter as wormwood
and as sharp as a double-edged sword.
Her feet go down to death;
her steps head straight for Sheol.
She doesn't consider the path of life;
she doesn't know that her ways are unstable.

Proverbs 5:3-6

Don't lust in your heart for her beauty
or let her captivate you with her eyelashes.
For a prostitute's fee is only a loaf of bread,
but the wife of another man goes after a precious life.
Can a man embrace fire
and his clothes not be burned?
Can a man walk on burning coals
without scorching his feet?
So it is with the one who sleeps with
another man's wife;
no one who touches her will go unpunished.
People don't despise the thief if he steals
to satisfy himself when he is hungry.
Still, if caught, he must pay seven times as much;
he must give up all the wealth in his house.
The one who commits adultery lacks sense;
whoever does so destroys himself.
He will get a beating and dishonor,
and his disgrace will never be removed.

For jealousy enrages a husband,
and he will show no mercy when he takes revenge.
He will not be appeased by anything
or be persuaded by lavish bribes.

Proverbs 6:25-35

At the window of my house
I looked through my lattice.
I saw among the inexperienced,
I noticed among the youths,
a young man lacking sense.
Crossing the street near her corner,
he strolled down the road to her house
at twilight, in the evening,
in the dark of the night.
A woman came to meet him
dressed like a prostitute,
having a hidden agenda.
She is loud and defiant;
her feet do not stay at home.
Now in the street, now in the squares,
she lurks at every corner.
She grabs him and kisses him;
she brazenly says to him,
"I've made fellowship offerings;
today I've fulfilled my vows.
So I came out to meet you,
to search for you, and I've found you.
I've spread coverings on my bed—
richly colored linen from Egypt.
I've perfumed my bed
with myrrh, aloes, and cinnamon.
Come, let's drink deeply of lovemaking until morning.
Let's feast on each other's love!
My husband isn't home;

he went on a long journey.
He took a bag of silver with him
and will come home at the time of the full moon."
She seduces him with her persistent pleading;
she lures with her flattering talk.
He follows her impulsively
like an ox going to the slaughter,
like a deer bounding toward a trap
until an arrow pierces its liver,
like a bird darting into a snare—
he doesn't know it will cost him his life.
Now, sons, listen to me,
and pay attention to the words from my mouth.
Don't let your heart turn aside to her ways;
don't stray onto her paths.
For she has brought many down to death;
her victims are countless.
Her house is the road to Sheol,
descending to the chambers of death.

Proverbs 7:6-27

The mouth of the forbidden woman is a deep pit;
a man cursed by the LORD will fall into it.

Proverbs 22:14

Theft

My son, if sinners entice you,
don't be persuaded.
If they say—"Come with us!
Let's set an ambush and kill someone.
Let's attack some innocent person just for fun!
Let's swallow them alive, like Sheol,
whole, like those who go down to the Pit.
We'll find all kinds of valuable property
and fill our houses with plunder.
Throw in your lot with us,
and we'll all share the loot"—
my son, don't travel that road with them
or set foot on their path,
because their feet run toward evil
and they hurry to shed blood.

Proverbs 1:10-16

It is useless to spread a net
where any bird can see it,
but they set an ambush to kill themselves;
they attack their own lives.
Such are the paths of all who make profit dishonestly;
it takes the lives of those who receive it.

Proverbs 1:17-19

Ill-gotten gains do not profit anyone,
but righteousness rescues from death.

Proverbs 10:2

Wealth obtained by fraud will dwindle,
but whoever earns it through labor will multiply it.

Proverbs 13:11

The one who profits dishonestly troubles his household,
but the one who hates bribes will live.

Proverbs 15:27

The one who plunders his father and evicts his mother
is a disgraceful and shameful son.

Proverbs 19:26

Food gained by fraud is sweet to a person,
but afterward his mouth is full of gravel.

Proverbs 20:17

Don't rob a poor person because he is poor,
and don't crush the oppressed at the city gate,
for the LORD will champion their cause
and will plunder those who plunder them.

Proverbs 22:22-23

The one who robs his father or mother
and says, "That's no sin,"
is a companion to a person who destroys.

Proverbs 28:24

To be a thief's partner is to hate oneself;
he hears the curse but will not testify.

Proverbs 29:24

Violence

My son, if sinners entice you,
don't be persuaded.
If they say—"Come with us!
Let's set an ambush and kill someone.
Let's attack some innocent person just for fun!
Let's swallow them alive, like Sheol,
whole, like those who go down to the Pit.
We'll find all kinds of valuable property
and fill our houses with plunder.
Throw in your lot with us,
and we'll all share the loot"—
my son, don't travel that road with them
or set foot on their path,
because their feet run toward evil
and they hurry to shed blood.

Proverbs 1:10-16

Don't envy a violent man
or choose any of his ways;
for the devious are detestable to the LORD,
but he is a friend to the upright.

Proverbs 3:31-32

For they can't sleep
unless they have done what is evil;
they are robbed of sleep
unless they make someone stumble.
They eat the bread of wickedness
and drink the wine of violence.

Proverbs 4:16-17

The LORD hates six things;
in fact, seven are detestable to him:
arrogant eyes, a lying tongue,
hands that shed innocent blood,
a heart that plots wicked schemes,
feet eager to run to evil,
a lying witness who gives false testimony,
and one who stirs up trouble among brothers.

Proverbs 6:16-19

Blessings are on the head of the righteous,
but the mouth of the wicked conceals violence.

Proverbs 10:6

The mouth of the righteous is a fountain of life,
but the mouth of the wicked conceals violence.

Proverbs 10:11

A gracious woman gains honor,
but violent people gain only riches.

Proverbs 11:16

From the fruit of his mouth,
a person will enjoy good things,
but treacherous people have an appetite for violence.

Proverbs 13:2

A violent person lures his neighbor,
leading him on a path that is not good.

Proverbs 16:29

The violence of the wicked sweeps them away
because they refuse to act justly.

Proverbs 21:7

Don't envy the evil
or desire to be with them,
for their hearts plan violence,
and their words stir up trouble.

Proverbs 24:1-2

Someone burdened by bloodguilt
will be a fugitive until death.
Let no one help him.

Proverbs 28:17

Bloodthirsty men hate an honest person,
but the upright care about him.

Proverbs 29:10

Wealth

My son, if you have put up security for your neighbor
or entered into an agreement with a stranger,
you have been snared by the words of your mouth
trapped by the words from your mouth.
Do this, then, my son, and free yourself,
for you have put yourself in your neighbor's power:

Go, humble yourself, and plead with your neighbor.
Don't give sleep to your eyes
or slumber to your eyelids.
Escape like a gazelle from a hunter,
like a bird from a hunter's trap.

Proverbs 6:1-5

With me [Wisdom] are riches and honor,
lasting wealth and righteousness.
My fruit is better than solid gold,
and my harvest than pure silver.
I walk in the ways of righteousness,
along the paths of justice,
giving wealth as an inheritance to those who love me,
and filling their treasuries.

Proverbs 8:18-21

The wealth of the rich is his fortified city;
the poverty of the poor is their destruction.

Proverbs 10:15

Wealth is not profitable on a day of wrath,
but righteousness rescues from death.

Proverbs 11:4

When the wicked person dies,
his expectation comes to nothing,
and hope placed in wealth vanishes.

Proverbs 11:7

If someone puts up security for a stranger,
he will suffer for it,
but the one who hates such agreements is protected.

Proverbs 11:15

Anyone trusting in his riches will fall,
but the righteous will flourish like foliage.

Proverbs 11:28

A lazy hunter doesn't roast his game,
but to a diligent person, his wealth is precious.

Proverbs 12:27

Riches are a ransom for a person's life,
but a poor person hears no threat.

Proverbs 13:8

Wealth obtained by fraud will dwindle,
but whoever earns it through labor will multiply it.

Proverbs 13:11

A good man leaves an inheritance to his grandchildren,
but the sinner's wealth is stored up for the righteous.

Proverbs 13:22

The crown of the wise is their wealth,
but the foolishness of fools produces foolishness.

Proverbs 14:24

The house of the righteous has great wealth,
but trouble accompanies the income of the wicked.

Proverbs 15:6

Better a little with the fear of the LORD
than great treasure with turmoil.

Proverbs 15:16

Better a little with righteousness
than great income with injustice.

Proverbs 16:8

One without sense enters an agreement
and puts up security for his friend.

Proverbs 17:18

The wealth of the rich is his fortified city;
in his imagination it is like a high wall.

Proverbs 18:11

Wealth attracts many friends,
but a poor person is separated from his friend.

Proverbs 19:4

Take his garment,
for he has put up security for a stranger;
get collateral if it is for foreigners.

Proverbs 20:16

An inheritance gained prematurely
will not be blessed ultimately.

Proverbs 20:21

Precious treasure and oil are in the dwelling of a wise
person,
but a fool consumes them.

Proverbs 21:20

A good name is to be chosen over great wealth;
favor is better than silver and gold.

Proverbs 22:1

Humility, the fear of the LORD,
results in wealth, honor, and life.

Proverbs 22:4

Don't be one of those who enter agreements,
who put up security for loans.
If you have nothing with which to pay,
even your bed will be taken from under you.

Proverbs 22:26-27

Don't wear yourself out to get rich;
because you know better, stop!
As soon as your eyes fly to it, it disappears,
for it makes wings for itself
and flies like an eagle to the sky.

Proverbs 23:4-5

Take his garment,
for he has put up security for a stranger;
get collateral if it is for foreigners.

Proverbs 27:13

Whoever increases his wealth through excessive interest
collects it for one who is kind to the poor.

Proverbs 28:8

A faithful person will have many blessings,
but one in a hurry to get rich
will not go unpunished.

Proverbs 28:20

A greedy one is in a hurry for wealth;
he doesn't know that poverty will come to him.

Proverbs 28:22

A man who loves wisdom brings joy to his father,
but one who consorts with prostitutes destroys his
wealth.

Proverbs 29:3

Give me neither poverty nor wealth;
feed me with the food I need.
Otherwise, I might have too much
and deny you, saying, "Who is the LORD?"
or I might have nothing and steal,
profaning the name of my God.

Proverbs 30:8b-9

Wickedness

For the upright will inhabit the land,
and those of integrity will remain in it;
but the wicked will be cut off from the land,
and the treacherous ripped out of it.

Proverbs 2:21-22

The LORD's curse is on the household of the wicked,
but he blesses the home of the righteous;

Proverbs 3:33

Keep off the path of the wicked;
don't proceed on the way of evil ones.
Avoid it; don't travel on it.
Turn away from it, and pass it by.
For they can't sleep
unless they have done what is evil;
they are robbed of sleep
unless they make someone stumble.
They eat the bread of wickedness
and drink the wine of violence.

Proverbs 4:14-17

The path of the righteous is like the light of dawn,
shining brighter and brighter until midday.

But the way of the wicked is like the darkest gloom;
they don't know what makes them stumble.

Proverbs 4:18-19

A worthless person, a wicked man
goes around speaking dishonestly,
winking his eyes, signaling with his feet,
and gesturing with his fingers.
He always plots evil with perversity in his heart;
he stirs up trouble.
Therefore calamity will strike him suddenly;
he will be shattered instantly, beyond recovery.

Proverbs 6:12-15

The remembrance of the righteous is a blessing,
but the name of the wicked will rot.

Proverbs 10:7

A sly wink of the eye causes grief,
and foolish lips will be destroyed.

Proverbs 10:10

The mouth of the righteous is a fountain of life,
but the mouth of the wicked conceals violence.

Proverbs 10:11

What the wicked dreads will come to him,
but what the righteous desire will be given to them.

Proverbs 10:24

When the whirlwind passes,
the wicked are no more,
but the righteous are secure forever.

Proverbs 10:25

The fear of the LORD prolongs life,
but the years of the wicked are cut short.

Proverbs 10:27

The hope of the righteous is joy,
but the expectation of the wicked will perish.

Proverbs 10:28

The righteous will never be shaken,
but the wicked will not remain on the earth.

Proverbs 10:30

The righteousness of the blameless clears his path,
but the wicked person will fall because of his wickedness.

Proverbs 11:5

The righteousness of the upright rescues them,
but the treacherous are trapped by their own desires.

Proverbs 11:6

When the wicked person dies,
his expectation comes to nothing,
and hope placed in wealth vanishes.

Proverbs 11:7

The righteous one is rescued from trouble;
in his place, the wicked one goes in.

Proverbs 11:8

When the righteous thrive, a city rejoices;
when the wicked die, there is joyful shouting.

Proverbs 11:10

A city is built up by the blessing of the upright,
but it is torn down by the mouth of the wicked.

Proverbs 11:11

The wicked person earns an empty wage,
but the one who sows righteousness, a true reward.

Proverbs 11:18

Genuine righteousness leads to life,
but pursuing evil leads to death.

Proverbs 11:19

Those with twisted minds are detestable to the LORD,
but those with blameless conduct are his delight.

Proverbs 11:20

Be assured that a wicked person
will not go unpunished,
but the offspring of the righteous will escape.

Proverbs 11:21

The desire of the righteous turns out well,
but the hope of the wicked leads to wrath.

Proverbs 11:23

If the righteous will be repaid on earth,
how much more the wicked and sinful.

Proverbs 11:31

One who is good obtains favor from the LORD,
but he condemns a person who schemes.

Proverbs 12:2

No one can be made secure by wickedness,
but the root of the righteous is immovable.

Proverbs 12:3

The thoughts of the righteous are just,
but guidance from the wicked is deceitful.

Proverbs 12:5

The words of the wicked are a deadly ambush,
but the speech of the upright rescues them.

Proverbs 12:6

The wicked are overthrown and perish,
but the house of the righteous will stand.

Proverbs 12:7

The righteous cares about his animal's health,
but even the merciful acts of the wicked are cruel.

Proverbs 12:10

The wicked desire what evil people have caught,
but the root of the righteous is productive.

Proverbs 12:12

By rebellious speech an evil person is trapped,
but a righteous person escapes from trouble.

Proverbs 12:13

Deceit is in the hearts of those who plot evil,
but those who promote peace have joy.

Proverbs 12:20

No disaster overcomes the righteous,
but the wicked are full of misery.

Proverbs 12:21

A righteous person is careful in dealing with his neighbor,
but the ways of the wicked lead them astray.

Proverbs 12:26

From the fruit of his mouth,
a person will enjoy good things,
but treacherous people have an appetite for violence.

Proverbs 13:2

The righteous hate lying,
but the wicked bring disgust and shame.

Proverbs 13:5

Righteousness guards people of integrity,
but wickedness undermines the sinner.

Proverbs 13:6

The light of the righteous shines brightly,
but the lamp of the wicked is put out.

Proverbs 13:9

A wicked envoy falls into trouble,
but a trustworthy courier brings healing.

Proverbs 13:17

Disaster pursues sinners,
but good rewards the righteous.

Proverbs 13:21

A righteous person eats until he is satisfied,
but the stomach of the wicked is empty.

Proverbs 13:25

The house of the wicked will be destroyed,
but the tent of the upright will flourish.

Proverbs 14:11

The evil bow before those who are good,
and the wicked, at the gates of the righteous.

Proverbs 14:19

The wicked one is thrown down by his own sin,
but the righteous one has a refuge in his death.

Proverbs 14:32

The sacrifice of the wicked is detestable to the LORD,
but the prayer of the upright is his delight.

Proverbs 15:8

The LORD detests the way of the wicked,
but he loves the one who pursues righteousness.

Proverbs 15:9

The LORD detests the plans of the one who is evil,
but pleasant words are pure.

Proverbs 15:26

The LORD is far from the wicked,
but he hears the prayer of the righteous.

Proverbs 15:29

The LORD has prepared everything for his purpose—
even the wicked for the day of disaster.

Proverbs 16:4

A worthless person digs up evil,
and his speech is like a scorching fire.

Proverbs 16:27

The one who narrows his eyes is planning deceptions;
the one who compresses his lips brings about evil.

Proverbs 16:30

A wicked person listens to malicious talk;
a liar pays attention to a destructive tongue.

Proverbs 17:4

An evil person desires only rebellion;
a cruel messenger will be sent against him.

Proverbs 17:11

A wicked person secretly takes a bribe
to subvert the course of justice.

Proverbs 17:23

When a wicked person comes, contempt also comes,
and along with dishonor, derision.

Proverbs 18:3

A worthless witness mocks justice,
and a wicked mouth swallows iniquity.

Proverbs 19:28

Whoever curses his father or mother—
his lamp will go out in deep darkness.

Proverbs 20:20

The violence of the wicked sweeps them away
because they refuse to act justly.

Proverbs 21:7

A guilty one's conduct is crooked,
but the behavior of the innocent is upright.

Proverbs 21:8

A wicked person desires evil;
he has no consideration for his neighbor.

Proverbs 21:10

The Righteous One considers the house of the wicked;
he brings the wicked to ruin.

Proverbs 21:12

The wicked are a ransom for the righteous,
and the treacherous, for the upright.

Proverbs 21:18

The sacrifice of a wicked person is detestable—
how much more so
when he brings it with ulterior motives!

Proverbs 21:27

A wicked person puts on a bold face,
but the upright one considers his way.

Proverbs 21:29

Don't set an ambush, you wicked one,
at the camp of the righteous man;
don't destroy his dwelling.
Though a righteous person falls seven times,
he will get up,
but the wicked will stumble into ruin.

Proverbs 24:15-16

Don't be agitated by evildoers,
and don't envy the wicked.
For the evil have no future;
the lamp of the wicked will be put out.

Proverbs 24:19-20

A righteous person who yields to the wicked
is like a muddied spring or a polluted well.

Proverbs 25:26

The wicked flee when no one is pursuing them,
but the righteous are as bold as a lion.

Proverbs 28:1

Those who reject the law praise the wicked,
but those who keep the law pit themselves against them.

Proverbs 28:4

Anyone who turns his ear away from hearing the law—
even his prayer is detestable.

Proverbs 28:9

When the righteous triumph,
there is great rejoicing,
but when the wicked come to power,
people hide.

Proverbs 28:12

When the righteous flourish, the people rejoice,
but when the wicked rule, people groan.

Proverbs 29:2

An evil person is caught by sin,
but the righteous one sings and rejoices.

Proverbs 29:6

The righteous person knows the rights of the poor,
but the wicked one does not understand these concerns.

Proverbs 29:7

When the wicked increase, rebellion increases,
but the righteous will see their downfall.

Proverbs 29:16

An unjust person is detestable to the righteous,
and one whose way is upright
is detestable to the wicked.

Proverbs 29:27

There is a generation that curses its father
and does not bless its mother.
There is a generation that is pure in its own eyes,
yet is not washed from its filth.
There is a generation—how haughty its eyes
and pretentious its looks.
There is a generation whose teeth are swords,
whose fangs are knives,

devouring the oppressed from the land
and the needy from among mankind.

Proverbs 30:11-14

This is the way of an adulteress:
she eats and wipes her mouth
and says, "I've done nothing wrong."

Proverbs 30:20

Wisdom

The proverbs of Solomon son of David, king of Israel:
For learning wisdom and discipline;
for understanding insightful sayings;
for receiving prudent instruction
in righteousness, justice, and integrity;
for teaching shrewdness to the inexperienced,
knowledge and discretion to a young man—
let a wise person listen and increase learning,
and let a discerning person obtain guidance—
for understanding a proverb or a parable,
the words of the wise, and their riddles.

Proverbs 1:1-6

Wisdom calls out in the street;
she makes her voice heard in the public squares.

She cries out above the commotion;
she speaks at the entrance of the city gates:
'How long, inexperienced ones, will you love ignorance?
How long will you mockers enjoy mocking
and you fools hate knowledge?
If you respond to my warning,
then I will pour out my spirit on you
and teach you my words.
Since I called out and you refused,
extended my hand and no one paid attention,
since you neglected all my counsel
and did not accept my correction,
I, in turn, will laugh at your calamity.
I will mock when terror strikes you,
when terror strikes you like a storm
and your calamity comes like a whirlwind,
when trouble and stress overcome you.
Then they will call me, but I won't answer;
they will search for me, but won't find me.
Because they hated knowledge,
didn't choose to fear the LORD,
were not interested in my counsel,
and rejected all my correction,
they will eat the fruit of their way
and be glutted with their own schemes.
For the apostasy of the inexperienced will kill them,
and the complacency of fools will destroy them.
But whoever listens to me will live securely
and be undisturbed by the dread of danger.'

Proverbs 1:20-33

My son, if you accept my words
and store up my commands within you,
listening closely to wisdom
and directing your heart to understanding;

furthermore, if you call out to insight
and lift your voice to understanding,
if you seek it like silver
and search for it like hidden treasure,
then you will understand the fear of the LORD
and discover the knowledge of God.

Proverbs 2:1-5

For the LORD gives wisdom;
from his mouth come knowledge and understanding.

Proverbs 2:6

Then you will understand righteousness, justice,
and integrity—every good path.
For wisdom will enter your heart,
and knowledge will delight you.

Proverbs 2:9-10

Happy is a man who finds wisdom
and who acquires understanding,
for she is more profitable than silver,
and her revenue is better than gold.
She is more precious than jewels;
nothing you desire can equal her.
Long life is in her right hand;
in her left, riches and honor.
Her ways are pleasant,
and all her paths, peaceful.
She is a tree of life to those who embrace her,
and those who hold on to her are happy.

Proverbs 3:13-18

The LORD founded the earth by wisdom
and established the heavens by understanding.
By his knowledge the watery depths broke open,
and the clouds dripped with dew.

Proverbs 3:19-20

Maintain sound wisdom and discretion.
My son, don't lose sight of them.
They will be life for you
and adornment for your neck.
Then you will go safely on your way;
your foot will not stumble.
When you lie down, you will not be afraid;
you will lie down, and your sleep will be pleasant.

Proverbs 3:21-24

Get wisdom, get understanding;
don't forget or turn away from the words from my
mouth.
Don't abandon wisdom, and she will watch over you;
love her, and she will guard you.
Wisdom is supreme—so get wisdom.

Proverbs 4:5-7a

I am teaching you the way of wisdom;
I am guiding you on straight paths.
When you walk, your steps will not be hindered;
when you run, you will not stumble.
Hold on to instruction; don't let go.
Guard it, for it is your life.

Proverbs 4:11-13

Say to wisdom, "You are my sister,"
and call understanding your relative.
She will keep you from a forbidden woman,
a wayward woman with her flattering talk.

Proverbs 7:4-5

Doesn't wisdom call out?
Doesn't understanding make her voice heard?
At the heights overlooking the road,
at the crossroads, she takes her stand.
Beside the gates leading into the city,

at the main entrance, she cries out:
"People, I call out to you;
my cry is to the children of Adam.
Learn to be shrewd, you who are inexperienced;
develop common sense, you who are foolish.
Listen, for I speak of noble things,
and what my lips say is right.
For my mouth tells the truth,
and wickedness is detestable to my lips.
All the words from my mouth are righteous;
none of them are deceptive or perverse.
All of them are clear to the perceptive,
and right to those who discover knowledge.
Accept my instruction instead of silver,
and knowledge rather than pure gold.
For wisdom is better than jewels,
and nothing desirable can equal it.
I, wisdom, share a home with shrewdness
and have knowledge and discretion.
To fear the LORD is to hate evil.
I hate arrogant pride, evil conduct,
and perverse speech.
I possess good advice and sound wisdom;
I have understanding and strength.
It is by me that kings reign
and rulers enact just law;
by me, princes lead,
as do nobles and all righteous judges.
I love those who love me,
and those who search for me find me.
With me are riches and honor,
lasting wealth and righteousness.
My fruit is better than solid gold,
and my harvest than pure silver.
I walk in the ways of righteousness,

along the paths of justice,
giving wealth as an inheritance to those who love me,
and filling their treasuries."

Proverbs 8:1-21

The LORD acquired me [Wisdom]
at the beginning of his creation,
before his works of long ago.
I was formed before ancient times,
from the beginning, before the earth began.
I was born
when there were no watery depths
and no springs filled with water.
Before the mountains were established,
prior to the hills, I was given birth—
before he made the land, the fields,
or the first soil on earth.
I was there when he established the heavens,
when he laid out the horizon on the surface of the
ocean,
when he placed the skies above,
when the fountains of the ocean gushed out,
when he set a limit for the sea
so that the waters would not violate his command,
when he laid out the foundations of the earth.
I was a skilled craftsman beside him.
I was his delight every day,
always rejoicing before him.
I was rejoicing in his inhabited world,
delighting in the children of Adam.

Proverbs 8:22-31

And now, sons, listen to me [Wisdom];
those who keep my ways are happy.
Listen to instruction and be wise;
don't ignore it.

Anyone who listens to me is happy,
watching at my doors every day,
waiting by the posts of my doorway.
For the one who finds me finds life
and obtains favor from the LORD,
but the one who misses me harms himself;
all who hate me love death.

Proverbs 8:32-36

Wisdom has built her house;
she has carved out her seven pillars.
She has prepared her meat; she has mixed her wine;
she has also set her table.
She has sent out her female servants;
she calls out from the highest points of the city:
"Whoever is inexperienced, enter here!"
To the one who lacks sense, she says,
"Come, eat my bread,
and drink the wine I have mixed.
Leave inexperience behind, and you will live;
pursue the way of understanding.
The one who corrects a mocker
will bring abuse on himself;
the one who rebukes the wicked will get hurt.
Don't rebuke a mocker, or he will hate you;
rebuke the wise, and he will love you.
Instruct the wise, and he will be wiser still;
teach the righteous, and he will learn more."

Proverbs 9:1-9

The fear of the LORD is the beginning of wisdom,
and the knowledge of the Holy One is understanding.
For by me your days will be many,
and years will be added to your life.

If you are wise, you are wise for your own benefit;
if you mock, you alone will bear the consequences.

Proverbs 9:10-12

Wisdom is found on the lips of the discerning,
but a rod is for the back of the one who lacks sense.

Proverbs 10:13

As shameful conduct is pleasure for a fool,
so wisdom is for a person of understanding.

Proverbs 10:23

When arrogance comes, disgrace follows,
but with humility comes wisdom.

Proverbs 11:2

The fruit of the righteous is a tree of life,
and a wise person captivates people.

Proverbs 11:30

A wise person's instruction is a fountain of life,
turning people away from the snares of death.

Proverbs 13:14

The one who walks with the wise will become wise,
but a companion of fools will suffer harm.

Proverbs 13:20

Every wise woman builds her house,
but a foolish one tears it down with her own hands.

Proverbs 14:1

The sensible person's wisdom is to consider his way,
but the stupidity of fools deceives them.

Proverbs 14:8

A wise person is cautious and turns from evil,
but a fool is easily angered and is careless.

Proverbs 14:16

The crown of the wise is their wealth,
but the foolishness of fools produces foolishness.

Proverbs 14:24

Wisdom resides in the heart of the discerning;
she is known even among fools.

Proverbs 14:33

A wise son brings joy to his father,
but a foolish man despises his mother.

Proverbs 15:20

The fear of the LORD is what wisdom teaches,
and humility comes before honor.

Proverbs 15:33

Get wisdom—
how much better it is than gold!
And get understanding—
it is preferable to silver.

Proverbs 16:16

Wisdom is the focus of the perceptive,
but a fool's eyes roam to the ends of the earth.

Proverbs 17:24

The words of a person's mouth are deep waters,
a flowing river, a fountain of wisdom.

Proverbs 18:4

Precious treasure and oil are in the dwelling of a wise
person,
but a fool consumes them.

Proverbs 21:20

A wise person went up against a city of warriors
and brought down its secure fortress.

Proverbs 21:22

Listen closely, pay attention to the words of the wise,
and apply your mind to my knowledge.
For it is pleasing if you keep them within you
and if they are constantly on your lips.
I have instructed you today—even you—

so that your confidence may be in the LORD.
Haven't I written for you thirty sayings
about counsel and knowledge,
in order to teach you true and reliable words,
so that you may give a dependable report
to those who sent you?

Proverbs 22:17-21

Buy—and do not sell—truth,
wisdom, instruction, and understanding.

Proverbs 23:23

The father of a righteous son will rejoice greatly,
and one who fathers a wise son will delight in him.
Let your father and mother have joy,
and let her who gave birth to you rejoice.

Proverbs 23:24-25

A house is built by wisdom,
and it is established by understanding;
by knowledge the rooms are filled
with every precious and beautiful treasure.

Proverbs 24:3-4

A wise warrior is better than a strong one,
and a man of knowledge than one of strength;
for you should wage war with sound guidance—
victory comes with many counselors.

Proverbs 24:5-6

Eat honey, my son, for it is good,
and the honeycomb is sweet to your palate;
realize that wisdom is the same for you.
If you find it, you will have a future,
and your hope will never fade.

Proverbs 24:13-14

Be wise, my son, and bring my heart joy,
so that I can answer anyone who taunts me.

Proverbs 27:11

The one who trusts in himself is a fool,
but one who walks in wisdom will be safe.

Proverbs 28:26

A man who loves wisdom brings joy to his father,
but one who consorts with prostitutes destroys his
wealth.

Proverbs 29:3

The glory of young men is their strength,
and the splendor of old men is gray hair.

Proverbs 20:29

Wonder

The leech has two daughters: "Give, Give!"
Three things are never satisfied;
four never say, "Enough!":
Sheol; a childless womb;
earth, which is never satisfied with water;
and fire, which never says, "Enough!"

Proverbs 30:15-16

Three things are too wondrous for me;
four I can't understand:
the way of an eagle in the sky,
the way of a snake on a rock,
the way of a ship at sea,
and the way of a man with a young woman.

Proverbs 30:18-19

The earth trembles under three things;
it cannot bear up under four:
a servant when he becomes king,
a fool when he is stuffed with food,
an unloved woman when she marries,
and a servant girl when she ousts her queen.

Proverbs 30:21-23

Four things on earth are small,
yet they are extremely wise:
ants are not a strong people,
yet they store up their food in the summer;
hyraxes are not a mighty people,
yet they make their homes in the cliffs;
locusts have no king,
yet all of them march in ranks;
a lizard can be caught in your hands,
yet it lives in kings' palaces.

Proverbs 30:24-28

Three things are stately in their stride;
four are stately in their walk:
a lion, which is mightiest among beasts
and doesn't retreat before anything;
a strutting rooster; a goat;
and a king at the head of his army.

Proverbs 30:29-31

Index